Ăn Chưa?

Simple Vietnamese Recipes
That Taste Like Home

Julie Mai Trần

Creator of Share My Roots

PAGE STREET
PUBLISHING CO.

First published in 2023 by

Page Street Publishing Co.

27 Congress Street, Suite 105

Salem, MA 01970

www.pagestreetpublishing.com

Distributed by Macmillan, sales in Canada by The Canadian Manda Group.

27   26   25   24   23   1   2   3   4   5

ISBN-13: 978-1-64567-943-1

ISBN-10: 1-64567-943-8

Library of Congress Control Number: 2022950289

Cover and book design by Molly Young for Page Street Publishing Co.

Photography by Julie Mai Trần

Printed and bound in the United States of America

To my parents
Linda Thu Mai and John Đức Trần,
Hoa Ái Hàng and Randy Quang Trần
and the Vietnamese Boat People

Cảm ơn má và ba đã hy sinh
cho các con.

*Amidst the shadows at dusk, filled with fear but armed with hope, my parents and
oldest sister escaped Việt Nam on a harrowing journey by boat in 1979.*

Original watercolor artwork by Thi Đoàn Art

Contents

Introduction

This cookbook will take you on a culinary adventure through the history and regions of Vietnam. My goal for this book is to celebrate Vietnam's past, present and future with authentic recipes that represent the country's culture, traditions and people. I hope when you try these recipes that they evoke feelings of nostalgia, bring you closer to your roots and welcome you to Vietnamese culture.

Món Việt (Vietnamese food) captures the essence of Vietnam's roots in all its glory—its diversity, cultural values, perseverance and achievements. It transcends time and connects people. Today, the Vietnamese diaspora has influenced all parts of the globe. Vietnamese food has easily gained popularity with such fan favorites as Phở, Bánh Mì, Gỏi Cuốn and Cà Phê Sữa Đá. However, we'll dig much deeper into Vietnamese gastronomy to explore a variety of must-try classics and lesser-known foods across Northern, Central and Southern Vietnam. Each of these regions boasts its own unique identity, reflected in distinct flavor profiles and cooking styles.

I envisioned this book to be a proud keepsake on your shelves used as a compass to navigate Vietnamese cooking, but also for some, to navigate home however you interpret the meaning of it. This piece of work is for my nieces, nephews and the next generation to keep in their hearts as they grow older. It is to honor my parents and in-laws, who inspire me. It is to recognize refugees and immigrants with similar but different stories. It is for the people who love Vietnamese food and the people behind it.

I am excited to share my roots through food! As you cook your way through this book, my hope is that you'll learn the fundamentals to master making your favorite dishes at home.

With love,

Exploring Family Roots Through Food

The development of this cookbook coincided with my personal journey that started five years ago to explore my culture and family history, which is intertwined with my love of food. Through this process, I learned deeply about my parents, my roots and *myself*.

My parents didn't have much while I was growing up, and yet we got to travel the world through Mom's cooking. She learned how to cook all types of international cuisines, turning common ingredients into something special. Perhaps the reason I'm drawn to cooking is that it reminds me of her love, compassion and strength. The kitchen and dining room were the heart of our home, and as Dad often says, she is the heart of our family.

I grew up in Orange County, California, home to a district called Little Saigon, which has one of the largest populations of the Vietnamese diaspora, with over 200,000 residents. People travel near and far to get to Little Saigon and experience a taste of Vietnam. Every weekend, I'd tag along on Mom's grocery trips there, where we'd find familiar faces, ingredients and language. On the bustling streets of Brookhurst, Bolsa and Westminster, you'll find family-owned Vietnamese restaurants, grocery markets and establishments tightly packed into plazas.

Despite Little Saigon's reputation as one of the best communities for Vietnamese food, we rarely ate out growing up because we had the luxury of Mom's home-cooked meals. Friends would ask me for the name of my favorite restaurant and I'd say, "Mom's kitchen." She bought groceries in bulk and stored them in her extra freezer right next to the American ingredients. It was clear that Mom wanted us to embrace our Vietnamese culture, too. After a long workday, she'd open the fridge and start experimenting on her Vietnamese favorites by memory of taste.

We knew it was a tough day at work when Dad's silence filled the air at the dinner table, his energy depleted. Nevertheless, he found solace in Mom's bowl of Phở and would give a sigh of relief. The silence was broken with Mom's contagious and vibrant energy. Dinner was a chance to pause from our fast-paced lives and be immersed in her cooking. The aroma of the Thịt Kho stewing brought back feelings of Vietnam (Việt Nam) for my parents while they created new feelings of what home meant for us kids.

Mom and Dad grew up during the Vietnam War, which lasted 20 years, almost their entire lives in Vietnam. In 1972, at the age of 24, Dad volunteered to fight for his country and led a group of 60 soldiers. The responsibility to lead these men safely weighed heavily on his shoulders. Every day, thousands of soldiers were dying and they didn't have resources to defend themselves. One day, a grenade landed where they were stationed, killing his comrades. He was badly injured; pieces of metal shards from the grenade were embedded in his leg. He tried to crawl somewhere safe and woke up after a successful surgery. Thankfully, he met my mother soon after and entered better days.

These stories were never conversation topics during dinner. Rather, they were raw memories for my parents that took decades to process and heal. As a kid and even an early adult, there was an unspoken understanding that my parents had suffered many losses—the loss of their home, family, friends and their former lives. Like many immigrant parents, mine lived in the present and the future. They never dwelled on the struggles of their past and rarely had time to reminisce about the good times. They focused on how to survive, adapt and provide for their family.

As Dad ate, I wondered whether his thoughts were about the constant pain he felt in his leg, the time he served in the war, his family in Vietnam or the friends that he lost in battle. As I found out over the years, what actually consumed his mind was how to make ends meet for his wife and three girls and shield us from worries.

My parents are now retired. One evening a few years ago, we gathered around the dining table, but this meal was different. Mom plated the Bánh Xèo and ladled the Nước Chấm. I reached for the herbs and hesitantly asked about their life in Vietnam. My questions took them by surprise. One question led to another and opened the door to more meaningful conversations. Each meal together thereafter became an opportunity to hear their stories, with food at the center of memories back in time.

On April 30, 1975, the fall of Saigon, South Vietnam's capital, to the North's communist forces marked the end of the Vietnam War. The North and South were reunified under a communist government. Within months, my parents got married and my older sister, Phương, was born a year later, but they had to make a plan because they feared for their lives. They were especially worried because Dad fought on the opposing side of the war. Being a Republic of Vietnam (RVN) soldier automatically incited undesirable attention and speculation by authorities. Those who had served in the South Vietnam military or government, and those who were successful business owners, were sent to "reeducation" prison camps for unknown periods of time. The prisoners were subjected to inhumane living conditions, hard labor, starvation, abuse and even persecution.

My parents escaped with my sister, who was two and a half years old. It took three attempts before they successfully found refuge. On their first attempt, Mom and my uncle Cậu Minh were scammed by a con artist as they waited by the water for their boat to arrive at dusk, to no avail.

On their second attempt, they left at dusk and hid below the boat's deck, crowded shoulder to shoulder, until they were out in the open, vast sea. On their journey, they faced multiple pirate attacks and their old wooden boat capsized. When they finally arrived in Thailand, they were turned away because the refugee camps were at capacity. They were stranded in the international sea for several days without food and fuel, until a Vietnamese fisherman brought them back to Vietnam on their ship.

The authorities stood on the sand and waited for the ship to dock. My mom and sister were imprisoned in a separate "reeducation" camp from my Dad for a few months. The overcrowded, unsanitary living conditions and harsh treatment drained them physically and mentally.

Despite their near-death experiences and knowing all too well the possible outcomes, they embarked on another escape on an old, worn wooden boat just days after Dad's release. There were only two trips left before the boat operation would shut down due to the increasing surveillance by authorities, so they took another chance.

This trip had its own heartaches, but they made it safely to Thailand. As they approached the shore, my parents worried they'd be turned away again.

Luckily, within months of their last escape, Thailand was given funding from the United Nations to accept additional refugees due to the alarming increase in numbers. "Boat 132" was the name of their campsite, representing the number of passengers onboard their boat. After living in Thailand for close to a year, they received clearance to resettle in America.

I asked them how they made this decision to flee, given all the risks. Mom looked at me, confused, and explained that the decision was simple: There was no other choice. In their case, they escaped not for a "better life" . . . *but to live at all*. Her answer put everything in perspective for me.

With hard work, determination and ongoing sacrifices, my parents gave their three daughters a life with opportunities they'd only dreamed were possible. They left their home and family in Vietnam, but they brought a piece of home to America through food. Although these memories were painful, there were moments of happiness sprinkled in during a tumultuous time.

"Between 1975 and 1992, almost two million Vietnamese risked their lives to flee oppression and hardship after the Vietnam War, in one of the largest mass exoduses in modern history. Escaping by boat, many found freedom in foreign land, many were captured and brutally punished and many did not survive the journey. This population of people are known as the Vietnamese Boat People."

—Vietnamese Boat People (vietnameseboatpeople.org)

Being a refugee and an immigrant doesn't define them, and the war doesn't define Vietnam. My parents had their own careers, hopes and dreams before and after immigrating to America. Food was the gateway to fonder memories of how they'd lived their lives as children, teenagers and adults who fell in love. They kept Vietnam in their hearts through eating Bánh Cuốn, from Mom's birthplace (Hà Nội) in the North; a bowl of Bún Bò Huế, hailing from Dad's hometown (Huế) in the Central region; and Bánh Mì, from Sài Gòn, where they met in the South. Each food is intertwined with the history and cultural traditions their parents passed down to them. These are the same traditions their kids revere until this day.

Every family has a story, and this one is ours. My parents' story represents hope, grit, determination and resilience. I hope this cookbook fosters a sense of community and pays tribute to other refugee and immigrant families.

We hope you enjoy our family recipes.

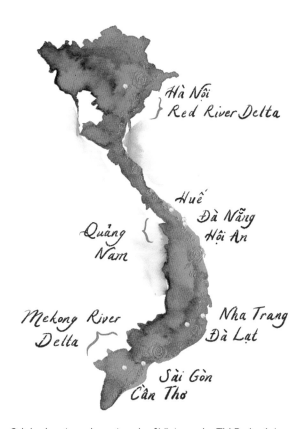

Original watercolor artwork of Vietnam by Thi Đoàn Art

Moms Don't Write Down Recipes

Well, they kind of do, but their version is much more nebulous . . . *or so we think*. A collection of scribbled notes written on a napkin, an ad in the mail or a free real estate notepad left at the front door were my mom and mother-in-law's version of a cookbook. And yet, they were sacred. Scan it, take a picture and don't lose those notes.

Perhaps the best lesson I've learned from Mom is how to adjust a recipe. Instead of a recipe, she would describe the ingredients and the process. *If it looks dry, add more water.* But what were these cryptic notes? I needed a recipe with the exact measurements and the exact steps taken. *"I just gave you the recipe,"* she said. Although I didn't know where to start at the time, now I hear Mom's voice in my head guiding me as I cook.

I wanted to know all the scenarios so I could get her recipes perfect the first time, but it took getting in the kitchen to truly understand the value of her notes. Cooking wasn't black and white. She shared what she thought really mattered because there are many variables at play. I've burnt my pan cooking the same dish using the same method that worked perfectly using another pan. That's because *cooking is dynamic*. You have to look for signs and adjust as needed.

Pots and stoves yield different results at the same setting; flours and starches dry out over time; and fish sauce brands vary in sodium. Mom uses all her senses—she notices the appearance, sounds, textures and tastes, and *then* decides what to do next.

My experience helping Mom cook, obsessively watching the Food Network and making my fair share of mistakes paid off as I documented her recipes and developed my own over the years. Mom cooked with her intuition, and now my own kicks in and tells me when my pan needs more oil or water; when the soup is boiling too rapidly; when to adjust the heat; whether I should add more fish sauce, salt or sugar; and whether the dough needs more water, flour or oil. As a first-generation Vietnamese Chinese American, millennial and foodie, I also couldn't help but challenge some of her methods. Did we have to parboil the meat and bones? Was it necessary to caramelize the sugar instead of adding it directly to the marinade? Couldn't we just combine the flours at the same time?

She didn't hesitate to humor her stubborn daughter. Once in a while, I'd find a great shortcut or an alternative method that delighted her. At other times, my curiosity led to a sticky disaster, *which also delighted her*. She would gracefully say, "That's okay, Con (an endearing Vietnamese word for "child"), let's do it again, the other way now."

With this cookbook, we struck a balance between authenticity and simplicity, providing a template for you to make the recipes as our family does, and the knowledge to make them your own.

Key Ingredients
for Vietnamese Cooking

Vietnamese cooking starts with having the essential ingredients as your foundation. Knowing where to start can be overwhelming, so I've outlined the ingredients I use most to cook spontaneously and capture the key flavors of Vietnamese cuisine. You don't need much to start cooking. My basic staples include a bottle of fish sauce, soy sauce, oyster sauce and hoisin sauce. A lot of umami magic can happen when these condiments are combined with sugar and aromatics such as shallots, garlic, onion and lemongrass. Fresh lime juice balances the richness of flavors while bird's eye chilies add spice and complexity. Finally, vinegar is a must for pickled vegetables. My kitchen is always stocked with these simple ingredients so I can cook Vietnamese food on a whim.

Sauces & Condiments

Fish Sauce (Nước Mắm)
This holy grail ingredient in Vietnamese cooking is used in place of salt for an umami flavor. It is made from salted, fermented anchovies that are pressed to achieve a dark, amber liquid. The brands I recommend include Việt Hương® and Phú Quốc, and for premium brands, Son® and Red Boat. Vegan "fish sauce" products are available online.

Soy Sauce (Xì Dầu)
Made from fermented soybeans and grains, this sauce is used for seasoning, marinades or dips. Regular soy sauce can be replaced with low-sodium soy sauce for less salt. The more viscous dark soy sauce adds color. I recommend brands such as Lee Kum Kee, Kimlan and Kikkoman®.

Oyster Sauce (Sốt Hàu)
This thick, dark amber sauce, extracted from oysters, was created by the founder of the brand Lee Kum Kee. It has a strong, savory, umami flavor. For a vegan replacement, use Lee Kum Kee's mushroom-flavored stir-fry sauce.

Hoisin Sauce (Tương Đen)
This is a fermented soybean paste blended with five-spice, sugar, garlic, vinegar, sesame oil and chiles. Used in marinades and glazes, it is sweeter than oyster sauce. My favorite is the Lee Kum Kee brand.

Vinegar (Giấm)
White distilled vinegar has the most acetic acid (5 to 8%), giving a sharp, tart flavor ideal for pickling vegetables.

Sriracha
Although originating in Thailand, this sauce is a Vietnamese regular. Most prominently known is the Huy Fong "rooster" brand. I recently discovered Chin-Su® brand chili sauce, which tastes in between a sweet chili and Sriracha sauce.

Chili Garlic Sauce (Tương Ớt Tỏi)
This creation by Huy Fong is used for marinades, dressings and as a condiment. It is similar to *sambal oelek*, an Indonesian chili paste made of crushed chiles, vinegar and salt, except it has a lot of garlic and other seasonings.

Sweet Chili Sauce (Tương Ớt Ngọt)
This sweet and tangy sauce is ideal for fried spring rolls or wontons. It can also enhance other sauces.

Cooking Oils
I mostly use a neutral cooking oil with a high smoking point, such as vegetable, grapeseed or avocado oil. Occasionally, to season, I use sesame oil (Dầu Mè), which has a strong, nutty aroma.

Crab Paste (Mắm Cua)
This paste consists of fermented crab innards and roe. It is often used for Bún Riêu (crab meatball noodle soup) and is a secret weapon for fillings and sauces. It is more subtle than fermented shrimp or anchovy paste. Pantai® brand is our go-to paste.

Fermented Shrimp Paste (Mắm Tôm)
This paste is made from salted, fermented dried, ground shrimp and has a bold, savory, briny flavor. A dollop will boost flavors of fillings, dips and soups.

Fermented Anchovy Paste (Mắm Nêm)
This pungent paste is made from salted and fermented anchovies, similar to fish sauce except it isn't strained. It is usually blended with pineapple when served as a dipping sauce.

Chấm Dipping Sauce
This women-owned brand has gained wide popularity as a new household favorite! This premixed dipping sauce is created with fresh ingredients, making it convenient to serve with your home-cooked meals.

Seasonings, Spices & Powders

Chicken and Mushroom Bouillon
This multipurpose powder is used to flavor soups, meats and vegetables. It is also often used for its MSG, although not all bouillon powders include it.

Chinese Five-Spice (Ngũ Vị Hương)
This potent powder includes Szechuan pepper, star anise, fennel seeds, cinnamon, cloves, ginger and/or coriander seeds. It uniquely represents the five elements of taste and is used for marinades or seasoning. Less is more with this spice, or it can be overpowering.

Star Anise (Hoa Hồi)
This spice is sweet with herbal and licorice notes, used to add a warm depth of flavor to soups or braises. As its name suggests, it looks like a star, with six to eight points. Each point has a small seed that holds the flavor. The whole star anise are discarded after use.

Fried Shallots (Hành Phi)
Sometimes labeled as "fried red onion," these are sold pre-fried or dried in a container or bag. Frying the dried instead of raw shallots can save a lot of time. French's® crispy fried onions are also a great emergency shortcut.

Annatto Seeds (Achiote)
These seeds are used to make annatto oil, which imparts a natural red-orange color and a subtle peppery and earthy flavor to fillings and soups.

Dried Shrimp (Tôm Khô)
Dried shrimp adds umami and sweetness to soups. They're also ground and toasted as a topping for Bánh. Find them in the international aisle of grocery stores or in the refrigerated aisle of Asian markets.

Monosodium Glutamate (MSG)
MSG powder enhances the umami of food. Its controversy is rooted in a racially based myth surrounding "Chinese restaurant syndrome," which positioned Asian food as "inferior and dirty." There is no scientific evidence that MSG causes health problems. It is naturally present in common foods, such as tomatoes and cheese. Although none of the recipes in this book require it, adding a pinch of MSG to marinades, stir-fries, soups, fillings and dips can elevate your dish's flavor.

Rock Sugar (Đường Phèn)
Made from sugarcane extract, rock sugar has a milder sweetness than refined sugar. It has no caramel under-tones, which makes it ideal for soups. For 1 inch (2.5 cm) of rock sugar, substitute 1½ teaspoons (7 g) of granulated sugar to start. For soups, I prefer to use yellow rock sugar, which is less refined, slightly sweeter and contains more nutrients.

Sea Salt (Muối Biển)
The type of salt used in the recipes throughout the book is sea salt, which is coarser and has less sodium than table salt. Adjust accordingly if using a different salt.

Aromatics & Herbs

Lemongrass (Sả)
A staple in Southeast Asian cuisine, lemongrass has a strong citrus taste without the bitterness or acid. The tender, center-cut pieces hold the flavor. Look for the preminced lemongrass in the frozen section of Asian markets, to save prep time. If you can't find lemongrass, the recipes are designed to be delicious even without it.

A lemongrass stalk is equivalent to 1 tablespoon (4 g) of minced lemongrass and can be substituted with 1 teaspoon of dried lemongrass if needed. Make sure there isn't added sodium if using the dried herb.

Preparation: Wash the lemongrass stalks, cut and remove the top 6 inches (15 cm) and bottom 1 to 2 inches (2.5 to 5 cm). Remove the thick, rough outer layers (at least two). The unused pieces may be dried and used for tea.

For flavoring soups, cut the stalks into three pieces, slice them in half and bruise them with a meat-tenderizing mallet. Gather the rough outer layers and tie the pieces together. For marinades, finely mince the center-cut pieces so they cook through. If using a food processor, preslice the lemongrass. If you pulse big chunks, it will be too fibrous, like a hairball.

Garlic, Shallots, Onions

These common aromatics are used throughout the book. Shallots have a mild, sweet flavor with complex garlic notes. Yellow onions have a more intense heat and retain their sharpness when cooked for long periods, ideal for soups. Green onions are versatile for topping, fillings or to make scallion oil.

Ginger, Limes, Bird's Eye Chiles

For common uses, I like to wash and store all of these whole in the freezer. When ready to use, rinse under cold water and prepare as usual. Ginger has a peppery, sweet and pungent taste that is often used in dishes with Chinese influence. The citrus of lime brightens up any dish, while the chiles add spice. If you can't find bird's eye chiles (also known as Thai chiles), use jalapeños.

Herbs (Rau Thơm)

Fresh herbs are important to complete the Vietnamese food experience, served on a platter at the table. They provide freshness and texture, and enhance other flavors. Tear off the leaves and add them whole to vermicelli bowls, rice plates and soups. In salads, the leaves may be left whole or rolled up and sliced. They can be eaten as an accompaniment or wrapped in lettuce with the main dish. What follows are descriptions of my favorite herbs.

Vietnamese coriander (Rau Răm) is slightly spicy and peppery, ideal for salads, soups and vermicelli bowls. *Perilla (Tía Tô)* leaves have a peppery and slightly bitter taste ideal for soups, grilled meats and Bánh. *Thai basil (Húng Quế)* has a licorice aroma used for Phở, other soups and salads. *Culantro* or *sawtooth (Ngò Gai)* tastes similar to cilantro except it has citrusy notes, ideal for Phở and Bánh. *Vietnamese balm (Kinh Giới)* has citrus, minty and bitter notes and is used for fresh spring rolls, soups, grilled meats and Bánh. Mint and cilantro are versatile for all the above. *Peppermint (Húng Cây)* is slightly spicy; *spearmint (Húng Lũi)* is slightly sweet.

The herbs that may be more widely available at the market are mint, *cilantro (Ngò)*, Thai basil and perilla leaves. In a pinch, you may use them interchangeably based on your preference.

Noodles

Fresh vs Dried

Fresh noodles, which retain a chewy texture, are located in the fridge aisle of most Asian markets, labeled "tươi" which means fresh. Dried noodles are convenient and work just as well. Unopened packages of dried noodles last a year. Store opened packages in an airtight container or ziplock bag. Egg noodles can be frozen and quickly thawed at room temperature in 30 minutes. In general, all noodles are best served al dente. Once cooked according to the package instructions, rinse them under cold water to stop them from overcooking, then coat with a few drops of neutral cooking oil to prevent sticking.

Rice Sticks (Bánh Phở)

Also labeled as "rice" or "Pad Thái" noodles, these are flat and come in widths ranging from S to XL. For soups, cook the dried noodles in boiling water for 7 to 9 minutes, depending on the size. Turn off the heat for 2 minutes, then rinse under cold water. For stir- or panfries, they may be soaked in warm water before cooking. For fresh noodles, quickly blanch them in boiling water for 10 seconds for soups, or give them a quick soak in room-temperature water according to directions before panfrying.

Rice Vermicelli Noodles (Bún)

These cylindrical noodles are made from rice and used for all dishes called Bún. These usually take 5 to 10 minutes to cook in boiling water. However, for Bún Bò Huế and Canh Bún soups, make sure to get the very thick, cylindrical vermicelli often labeled "Bún Bò Huế" noodles. These take up to 20 minutes to cook in boiling water.

Noodles (continued)

Fine Rice Vermicelli Stacks (Bánh Hỏi)

These fine cylindrical noodles are weaved into rectangular stacks for a bouncy texture. They can be used as an alternative to Bún and cook in boiling water for 1 to 1½ minutes.

Mung Bean Thread, Cellophane or Glass Noodles (Miến)

Made of mung bean starch, these noodles turn translucent and chewy when cooked. The finer noodles, labeled "Bún Tàu," are often soaked in water for 20 minutes, drained and used in fillings. Noodles labeled "Miến Dong" are thicker and used in soups and stir-fries.

Tapioca Noodles (Bánh Canh)

These thick, chewy noodles are made of tapioca and sometimes rice flour. They are similar to Japanese *udon* noodles and are most commonly used in soups.

Egg Noodles (Mì)

These are made from egg and wheat flour and originate from China. Wonton and egg noodles are springy and ideal for soups or saucy stir-fries. They may come presteamed or dried, and they cook within 1 minute in boiling water. The dried version is great for deep-frying to make a fried bird's nest, as in Crispy Fried Noodles (page 127).

Rice, Starches & Dried Goods

Rice (Gạo) and Sticky Rice (Gạo Nếp)

Jasmine rice is Vietnam's staple crop, grown in southern Vietnam. Glutinous rice, known as sweet rice, is used for sticky rice (Xôi) in savory and sweet dishes. Rinse the rice before cooking to remove excess starches. This prevents the grains from clumping together when cooked.

Flours and Starches (Bột)

Different ratios of flours and starches create batters and doughs with various consistencies in Vietnamese cooking. Rice flour yields a soft texture for such dishes as steamed rice cakes and sizzling crêpes. Glutinous rice flour yields a sticky, mochi-like texture used for such foods as sticky rice dumplings. Tapioca starch is often added to rice flour to create a chewier texture used for such items as steamed rice rolls. Potato starch is more delicate than rice flour and is used to make doughs or batters less dense and soft. All-purpose flour offers a coarser grain that creates a firmer texture in such foods as steamed buns and bread. Cornstarch is used as a thickener, as a meat tenderizer and to crisp up batters.

Dried Wood Ear Mushrooms (Mộc Nhĩ Khô)

Also known as black fungus, these have a wavy earlike shape, a crunchy jelly texture and an earthy flavor. They are available, whole or sliced, in plastic packages. Soak them in warm water for 20 minutes, drain, then chop them to use in fillings.

Rice Paper (Bánh Tráng)

These translucent, edible sheets are made from rice and water. They are rehydrated with water to make pliable for wrapping Gỏi Cuốn. The dried rice paper can also be fried or grilled on a pan for Vietnamese street pizza.

Vietnamese Coffee (Cà Phê)

Vietnam is the world's second-largest coffee producer, and the largest producer of Robusta beans. Such companies as Nam Coffee, Nguyen Coffee Supply, Omni and Sang are putting Vietnamese coffee beans on the map and raising the visibility of the country's farmers.

Storage Tips

Store opened packages of dried goods in an airtight container placed in a cool area, to preserve their shelf life and quality. I highly recommend freezing bags of rice and flour for four days after purchase. This kills insect eggs and larvae (if present) and prevents such pests as grain weevils from invading your pantry. Let the bags come down to room temperature and store them in an airtight container.

arious dried noodles and rice paper

Various ingredients found in the frozen section of Asian markets

Fresh noodles found in the refrigerated section of Asian markets

Vegetarian or Vegan Options

Marinades or stir-fries can be made vegan by replacing meat proteins. Substitute firm tofu and king oyster mushrooms for a meaty texture. The cooking times and amount of marinade will need to be adjusted. Dry the tofu by wrapping it with cheesecloth and gently pressing out the liquid. Slice the king oyster mushrooms into thick coins and score them in a tic-tac-toe shape to help them absorb flavor and cook evenly through. For condiments, replace chicken bouillon powder with mushroom or vegetarian bouillon powder; replace oyster sauce with vegetarian stir-fry sauce or hoisin sauce; and try Yondu Seasoning brand as a substitute for fish sauce. Check out the Vegan Nước Chấm (page 179) and All-Purpose Vegan Mushroom Filling and Topping (page 111), which are versatile for many of the recipes in this book.

Tools

Large Nonstick Skillet
For the recipes in this book, I'm mostly using a 12-inch (30-cm) nonstick skillet with deep sides, which gives me a large surface area to cook large portions without over-crowding the ingredients.

Stockpot
For making large quantities of soups, braises and stews, I recommend using at least an 8-quart (8-L) stockpot. However, the ideal size is a 12-quart (11-L) stockpot to give you ample space.

Steamer
A 10- to 12-inch (25- to 30-cm) steamer is a good size for the recipes in this book that require steaming. If you don't have a steamer, use a large pot, deep skillet or wok. Place an inverted heatproof bowl, or balls of foil, on top to use as a rack. Fill the makeshift steamer with water no more than 1 inch (2.5 cm) below the top of the "rack." Bring the water to a boil over medium-high heat. Place what needs to be steamed in a heatproof dish on top of the rack and cover with a lid. Adjust the heat as necessary. There needs to be enough water to generate steam without its boiling over into the food. If the food steams for a long period of time, check periodically to see whether the water needs to be refilled.

Ăn Cơm Chưa?

Bún and Cơm Đĩa
(Vermicelli and Rice Dishes)

"Ăn Cơm Chưa," which translates to "Have you eaten (rice), yet?" is the first thing my parents will ask me when I visit . . . and I'll feel at home. Before I can answer, Mom will hurry to the kitchen and begin clattering away. She'll bring to the dining table several dishes that she spent all morning preparing. Even when my parents were busy, we never missed a meal together.

In this expression, the important role of rice in Vietnam's economy and livelihood is highlighted, although the word *rice* isn't used in the literal sense. This greeting is similar to the phrase "How are you?" and holds a deeper meaning with its warmer nuance in Vietnamese culture. When I come over to my in-laws or my best friend's home, I am greeted the same way. Care and consideration are often shown through nourishment.

Assimilation had its challenges. My parents had to start their lives over in another country, in another language, with a kid, and during a very controversial time. They were a part of the second wave of Vietnamese refugees who came to America after the war, in the midst of a recession. By this time, many considered Vietnamese refugees an economic burden and the resentment showed through hostile remarks and broken eggshells on their yolk-stained car windows. Fortunately, they also met kind people along the way who gave them hope. Regardless of their daily struggles, Mom cranked out dinner in no time. In Vietnam, dinnertime was the only time her parents, brothers and sisters could come together during their busy schedules, and she wanted that bonding time for our family.

Most of the recipes in this chapter are ideal for weeknight cooking or for meal prepping. I recommend marinating meats overnight to fully absorb the flavor. This also breaks down the cooking process and makes it manageable to cook after work. Plan ahead and make certain condiments, such as pickled vegetables and fried shallots, in advance for the month. Sliced fresh lettuce, cucumbers and tomatoes make an effortless side. Sauces, such as Nước Chấm, can be made ahead, frozen and quickly reheated for use.

Browning meat and vegetables gives them a distinctive flavor, aroma and color via the Malliard reaction. This chemical reaction produces hundreds of flavor compounds, which is why you want to avoid overcrowding pans if you're trying to brown or sear something. Deglazing the pan with 1 tablespoon (15 ml) of water at a time can prevent marinades from burning while the meat finishes cooking. I always have a cup (240 ml) of water nearby when cooking marinated meats or vegetables in a pan. These tips can take your results to the next level.

Finally, rice vermicelli bowls and rice plates can be as simple or intricate as you wish. Mix and match the proteins with rice, vermicelli, lettuce or rice paper to create your own noodle bowl, rice plate, salad or fresh spring rolls. Refer to the final chapter, "The Essentials: Sauces, Dips and Condiments" (page 177), for ideas on sides, toppings and dressings.

Grilled BBQ Pork and Shrimp (Bún Tôm Thịt Nướng)

If I had to pick my favorite Vietnamese dish, this would be it. When I was young, I didn't care for rice, so Mom would make me Bún Tôm Thịt Nướng. It opened my eyes to the beauty of Vietnamese cuisine. The rice vermicelli is topped with grilled caramelized pork and shrimp, pickled carrots and daikon, fried shallots, roasted peanuts, scallion oil and herbs with Nước Chấm. To me, this dish represents key aspects of Vietnamese cooking, including caramelization, pickling, texture and a balance of flavors—savory, sweet, sour, spicy and bitter. Although I enjoy the combination of grilled pork and shrimp, feel free to make just one or the other, if you prefer.

Yield: 6 servings

Grilled BBQ Pork

1 head garlic, minced

¼ cup (17 g) finely minced fresh lemongrass

½ cup (100 g) sugar

2 tbsp (30 ml) fish sauce

1 tbsp (15 ml) soy sauce

1½ tsp (8 ml) oyster sauce

Pinch of freshly ground black pepper

¼ cup (60 ml) neutral oil, divided, if panfrying, or 2 tbsp (30 ml) if air frying

3 lb (1.4 kg) pork shoulder or butt

Cooking oil spray, if air frying

Grilled BBQ Shrimp

1 tsp fish sauce

1½ tsp (8 ml) honey or (5 g) sugar

½ large shallot, minced

3 cloves garlic, minced

Pinch of freshly ground black pepper

8 oz (225 g) shrimp, peeled and deveined

1 to 2 tbsp (15 to 30 ml) neutral cooking oil

For Serving

1½ lb (680 g) dried rice vermicelli noodles, cooked

Scallion Oil (page 180)

Pickled Carrots and Daikon (page 182)

Fresh lettuce, mint, perilla leaves

2 large English cucumbers, julienned

Nước Chấm (page 178)

2 limes, cut into 4 wedges

Marinate the Pork: In a large bowl, combine the garlic, lemongrass, sugar, fish sauce, soy sauce, oyster sauce, pepper and 2 tablespoons (30 ml) of the oil. Slice the pork into about 2 x 3–inch (5 x 7.5–cm) pieces that are ⅛ inch (3 mm) thick. Add the slices of pork to the bowl and coat them well. Cover and marinate in the fridge for at least 2 hours, ideally overnight for best results.

Panfry Method: In a large skillet, heat the remaining 2 tablespoons (30 ml) of oil over medium-high heat. You will be cooking the pork in two batches—do not overcrowd the pan, or the pork will steam instead of brown. Add half of the pork in a single layer and cook undisturbed to get a nice char. After the pork has browned on the first side, 2 to 3 minutes, flip the pork over. Add 1 to 2 tablespoons (15 to 30 ml) of water to deglaze the pan and prevent the pork from burning. Continue to cook for 2 to 3 minutes. This will also help give the meat an even color. In between batches, add water and wipe down the pan, if needed. Cook the second batch of pork.

Air Fryer Method: Preheat an air fryer for 10 minutes at 375°F (190°C). Spray the tray with cooking oil and place the pork in a single layer. Cook in batches and do not overcrowd the tray, or the pork will steam instead of brown. Air fry the pork for 6 minutes at 375°F (190°C), then flip the pieces over and cook at 385°F (196°C) for 6 minutes. The temperature and timing may vary by air fryer.

Marinate the Shrimp: In a large bowl, combine the fish sauce, honey, shallot, garlic and pepper. Add the shrimp and coat them well.

Panfry the Shrimp: In a large skillet, heat the oil over medium-high heat. Add the shrimp in a single layer and cook for 1½ minutes, then flip and cook for 1½ minutes. Add 1 tablespoon (15 ml) of water to deglaze the pan and prevent the marinade from burning. Swirl the pan around and transfer the shrimp to a bowl.

Serve: Plate the grilled pork and shrimp over rice vermicelli noodles and top with scallion oil, pickled carrots and daikon, herbs, cucumber, Nước Chấm and a lime wedge.

Lemongrass Chicken Thighs (Gà Nướng Sả)

Lemongrass chicken is perhaps the most popular recipe on my blog. It is simple to make on a weeknight, yet it feels indulgent, like a weekend meal. It is very important to finely chop the lemongrass so that the flavors can absorb into the chicken and cook through. Otherwise, you'll end up chomping on hay, wondering about the appeal of lemongrass. Although fresh is best, I like to stock up on frozen minced lemongrass from Asian markets and store it in the freezer for easy, flavorful cooking.

Yield: 6 servings

6 to 10 cloves garlic, minced

2 shallots, chopped

¼ cup (17 g) fresh minced lemongrass

¼ cup (60 g) light or dark brown sugar

3 tbsp (45 ml) fish sauce

1 tbsp (15 ml) soy sauce

3 tbsp (45 ml) fresh lime juice

9 to 12 skin-on chicken thighs (3 to 4 lb [1.4 to 1.8 kg] boneless, or 5 lb [2.3 kg] bone-in)

2 tbsp (30 ml) vegetable oil, for baking sheet, if using oven method

Cooking oil spray, if air frying

For Serving

1½ lb (680 g) dried rice vermicelli noodles, cooked

Lettuce, sliced

Scallion Oil (page 180)

Pickled Carrots and Daikon (page 182)

Nước Chấm (page 178)

2 limes, cut into 4 wedges

Marinate the Chicken: In a large bowl, combine the garlic, shallots, lemongrass, brown sugar, fish sauce, soy sauce and lime juice. Clean the chicken, trim the skin and pat dry. Add the chicken to the bowl and coat it well, not forgetting to coat under the skin. Cover and marinate in the fridge for at least 6 hours, ideally overnight for best results.

Remove from the fridge 30 minutes before cooking to bring it to room temperature for even cooking. When thoroughly cooked, the chicken thighs should reach 165°F (73°C).

Oven Method: Line a large baking sheet with aluminum foil. Brush the foil with the oil and add the thighs, skin side up. Bake at 400°F (200°C) for 20 to 22 minutes on the middle rack. By this time, the skin will look lackluster. To get the "grilled, charbroiled effect," transfer the pan one rack higher and broil for 3 to 5 minutes. Carefully watch it and remove the chicken before the marinade on the skin burns. For bone-in chicken thighs, cook 5 minutes longer before broiling.

Air Fryer Method: Preheat an air fryer for 5 minutes. Spray the tray with cooking oil.

Boneless chicken thighs: Air fry at 380°F (193°C) for 15 to 18 minutes, skin side up.

Bone-in chicken thighs: Air fry at 380°F (193°C) for 20 minutes, skin side up.

Serve: Let the chicken rest for 5 minutes, then slice and plate it over rice vermicelli noodles and lettuce. Top with scallion oil, pickled carrots and daikon, Nước Chấm and a lime wedge.

Beef Stir-Fry (Bún Bò Xào)

Bún Bò Xào originated in Hanoi and is known as Bún Bò Nam Bộ in the South. This is a quick and easy dish to make, and it's a great recipe for cheaper cuts of beef. My mother-in-law's secret for tenderizing chewy cuts of beef, such as chuck roast or round steak, is to add ¼ peeled kiwi per pound (455 g) of beef to the marinade for at least an hour. The kiwi has enzymes that help break down the muscle fibers in the protein quickly, while the neutral flavor blends in naturally with the marinade. A little kiwi pulp goes a long way, and too much can result in mushy meat. Alternatively, you can use 1 teaspoon of cornstarch.

Yield: 6 servings

2 tbsp (26 g) sugar

2 tbsp (30 ml) fish sauce

2 tbsp (30 ml) oyster sauce

1 tsp dark soy sauce

1 head garlic, minced

¼ cup (17 g) finely minced fresh lemongrass (optional)

Pulp of ½ kiwi, or 1 tsp cornstarch (optional for chewy cuts of beef)

3 tbsp (45 ml) neutral cooking oil, divided

2 lb (905 g) beef (sirloin, flank steak, top round or chuck roast)

1 large yellow onion, sliced

For Serving

1½ lb (680 g) dried rice vermicelli noodles, cooked

Lettuce, sliced

Fresh cilantro, mint, perilla leaves

Pickled Carrots and Daikon (page 182)

Crushed toasted peanuts

Nước Chấm (page 178)

2 limes, cut into wedges

Marinate the Beef: In a large bowl, combine the sugar, fish sauce, oyster sauce, dark soy sauce, garlic, lemongrass (if using), kiwi and 1 tablespoon (15 ml) of the oil. Slice the beef perpendicularly across the grain into thin strips 3 inches (7.5 cm) long. If needed, freeze the beef for 10 minutes to make it easier to slice thinly. Place the beef slices in the bowl and coat them well. Cover and marinate in the fridge for at least 1 hour, ideally overnight for best results.

Panfry the Beef: In a large skillet, heat 1 tablespoon (15 ml) of the oil over medium-high heat and sauté the onion until softened, about 4 minutes. Move the onion to the perimeter of the pan and add the remaining tablespoon (15 ml) of oil to the center. You will be cooking the beef in two batches—don't overcrowd the pan, or the beef will steam instead of brown. Increase the heat to high, add half of the beef in a single layer and let it sear undisturbed for 1 to 2 minutes. Flip the pieces of beef over and cook for 1 to 2 minutes undisturbed. Finally, give the beef and onion a final toss in the pan, then remove and set aside. If the marinade cooks too quickly, add 1 tablespoon (15 ml) of water to deglaze the pan and prevent it from burning. Cook the remaining beef.

Serve: Plate the beef and onion mixture over rice vermicelli noodles and lettuce. Top with herbs, pickled carrots and daikon, crushed toasted peanuts, Nước Chấm and a wedge of lime.

Shrimp Paste Lemongrass Skewers (Chạo Tôm)

These skewers are inspired by Chạo Tôm, a shrimp paste that is typically wrapped around a sugarcane stick. This tasty snack originates from Huế in Central Vietnam. These skewers can be served as an appetizer or as an add-on item for special combination vermicelli bowls or broken rice plates. The paste is seasoned with garlic, fish sauce and lemongrass. Since sugarcane can be difficult to find, I'm replacing it in this recipe with lemongrass stalks. However, you can also form the mixture into patties without placing them on skewers.

Yield: 8 skewers

3 lemongrass stalks

1 lb (455 g) shrimp, peeled and deveined

1½ tsp (8 ml) fish sauce

2 tsp (9 g) sugar

1½ tbsp (12 g) cornstarch, plus more if needed

½ tsp baking powder

2 cloves garlic, minced

¼ cup (33 g) finely diced jicama (optional)

½ cup (30 g) panko bread crumbs

1 large egg, separated

Neutral cooking oil

For Serving

Lettuce

Nước Chấm (page 178)

1 lb (455 g) dried rice vermicelli noodles, cooked, or rice (optional)

Prepare the Lemongrass: Wash the lemongrass stalks thoroughly. Remove the outer two layers of the stalks and cut those layers into 6-inch (15-cm)-long pieces to serve as your "skewers." Finely mince the center-cut pieces of the stalk and set aside for the shrimp paste mixture. You should end up with 3 tablespoons (13 g) of minced lemongrass. If you can't find lemongrass, you may also form the shrimp paste into patties or wrap it around thick wooden skewers that have been presoaked for 15 minutes.

Prepare the Shrimp Paste: Pat the shrimp dry and grind them in a food processor, or use your knife to finely mince them, until they become a paste. In a large bowl, mix together the minced shrimp, minced lemongrass, fish sauce, sugar, cornstarch, baking powder, garlic and jicama. Gently fold in the panko bread crumbs. In a small bowl, whisk the egg white vigorously until foamy, then gently fold it into the paste.

Refrigerate the mixture for 15 minutes. To shape, add a few drops of oil to your hands to prevent the paste from sticking to them. Divide the shrimp paste into eight equal portions. Press the mixture around the lemongrass stalks, leaving at least 2 inches (5 cm) of the stalk sticking out at one end to use as a handle. The paste should be ½ inch (1.3 cm) thick around the lemongrass stalk. If the paste falls apart when forming its shape with your hands, add more cornstarch to bind it together. Brush the egg yolk sparingly but evenly on the outside of the shrimp mixture.

Panfry the Skewers: In a large skillet, heat a 1-inch (2.5-cm) depth of oil over medium-high heat. Once the oil is hot, cook the skewers for about 1½ minutes per side, rotating them to cook evenly until golden.

Serve: Enjoy the skewers with lettuce and dip into Nước Chấm. Optionally, serve with cooked rice vermicelli noodles or rice.

Vietnamese Grilled Pork Meatballs (Bún Chả Hà Nội)

These flavorful, juicy meat patties have garnered media attention worldwide after being featured on Anthony Bourdain's Parts Unknown *with an appearance by former president Barack Obama. Originating in Hanoi, this popular dish consists of charcoal-grilled pork patties or meatballs served with rice vermicelli noodles and Nước Chấm. It is served two different ways. Some like to eat the pork directly in what is referred to as the fish sauce broth and dunk a side of vermicelli into the bowl. The other way to eat it is more typical of vermicelli bowls, in which the concentrated sweet fish sauce is used as a dressing.*

Yield: 12 to 14 patties

Pork Patties

1 lb (455 g) ground pork

1 tbsp (15 g) light or dark brown sugar

1½ tsp (8 ml) honey

1½ tbsp (23 ml) fish sauce

1 tsp oyster sauce

3 cloves garlic, minced

2 shallots, chopped

2 tbsp (9 g) finely minced lemongrass (optional)

3 green onions, sliced (whites only)

2 tbsp (30 ml) neutral oil, if panfrying

Cooking oil spray, if air frying

Nước Chấm

¾ cup (175 ml) warm water (110°F [43°C])

¼ cup (50 g) sugar

¼ cup (60 ml) fish sauce

6 cloves garlic, minced

3 bird's eye chiles, sliced and seeded (optional)

Juice of 2 limes

Additional 2 cups (475 ml) water, if serving "broth style"

For Serving

1½ lb (680 g) dried rice vermicelli noodles, cooked

Fresh lettuce, mint, perilla leaves

Scallion Oil (page 180)

Pickled Carrots and Daikon (page 182)

Marinate the Pork Patties: In a large bowl, combine the ground pork, brown sugar, honey, fish sauce, oyster sauce, garlic, shallots, lemongrass (if using) and white parts of the green onions. Allow the mixture to rest for 15 minutes. Form 1½-inch (4-cm) meatballs and flatten each slightly into a patty so they cook evenly. This recipe will yield 12 to 14 patties.

Cook the Pork Patties: The internal temperature should reach 165°F (73°C) for cooked pork patties.

Panfry Method: In a large skillet, heat the 2 tablespoons (30 ml) of neutral oil over medium heat. You will be cooking the patties in two batches—don't overcrowd the pan, or the meat will steam instead of brown. Cook half of the patties in a single layer. After the pork has begun to brown on the first side, 1 to 2 minutes, add 1 tablespoon (15 ml) of water to deglaze the pan and prevent the marinade from burning. Continue to cook for 2 minutes. This will also help give the meat an even color. Flip the patties and cook for 4 minutes. Add 1 tablespoon (15 ml) of water to deglaze the pan whenever the marinade cooks too fast. In between batches, add water and wipe down the pan, if needed.

Air Fryer Method: Preheat an air fryer to 350°F (180°C) for 5 minutes. Spray the tray with cooking oil. Air fry the meatballs in a single layer for 5 minutes. Flip and air fry for 5 minutes, but adjust the time as needed based on your air fryer.

Make the Nước Chấm: In a small bowl, combine the warm water, sugar, fish sauce, garlic, bird's eye chiles and lime juice. To serve the patties in a "broth style," transfer the Nước Chấm to a medium-sized pot, add the additional 2 cups (475 ml) of water and warm the "broth" over the stove.

Serve: Plate the pork patties over rice vermicelli noodles and herbs. Top with scallion oil and serve with a side of Nước Chấm and pickled carrots and daikon. Alternatively, serve the Nước Chấm "broth" in individual bowls for guests to submerge their patties and dip their noodles and herbs.

Vietnamese Grilled Pork Sausage (Nem Nướng)

Mom grills these sweet, savory and smoky sausages for special occasions! We like to wrap them in a fresh spring roll. The sausages are a specialty of Nha Trang, on the South Central coast. They have a springy texture from the baking powder that puffs up the meat while it cooks. If you're feeling advanced, add the pork fatback, which is a hard, firmer type of fat that adds to the sausage's bouncy texture. It is often found attached to a pork loin. Boiling the diced fat provides a unique texture when you bite into the sausage, bursting with juice and flavor. However, it isn't required and these will be a hit either way.

Yield: 4 servings

Pork Paste

1½ lb (680 g) ground pork, 80% lean

4 oz (113 g) pork fatback, diced finely (optional)

1½ to 1⅔ tbsp (20 to 24 g) sugar

6 cloves garlic, minced

2 large shallots, minced

1½ tbsp (23 ml) fish sauce

1½ tbsp (23 ml) hoisin sauce

1½ tbsp (23 ml) honey

2 tbsp (30 ml) Annatto Oil (page 181) or neutral oil

1 tbsp (15 ml) water

1 tbsp (8 g) cornstarch

1½ tsp (8 ml) Shaoxing wine

1½ tsp (3 g) ground black pepper

1 tsp paprika

½ tsp baking powder

½ tsp five-spice powder

¼ tsp salt

2 tbsp (30 ml) neutral oil, for panfrying

Glaze

1½ tbsp (23 ml) oyster sauce

1 tbsp (15 ml) soy sauce

1 tbsp (15 ml) honey

1 tbsp (15 ml) water

1 tbsp (15 ml) Annatto Oil (page 181) or neutral cooking oil

For Serving

2 lb (905 g) dried fine rice vermicelli (Bánh Hỏi), cooked

Fresh lettuce, perilla leaves

Peanut Sauce (page 183)

Make the Pork Paste: Freeze the ground pork for no longer than 1 hour. It should be chilled (not hard frozen) to maintain its firm texture when being blended. This will keep the integrity of the fat visually separate in the sausage.

If using, bring a small pot of water to a boil, cook the diced pork fat for 2 minutes, then rinse under cold water. Coat the fat with 1 teaspoon of the sugar and let it cool.

In a large bowl, combine the garlic, shallots, fish sauce, hoisin sauce, 1½ tablespoons (20 g) of sugar, honey, annatto oil, water, cornstarch, Shaoxing wine, pepper, paprika, baking powder, five-spice powder and salt to make a marinade. In a food processor, blend the slightly frozen pork with the marinade until it becomes a paste, 30 seconds to 1 minute. Add the boiled pork fat and pulse it for 30 seconds. Transfer the paste to a ziplock bag or bowl and refrigerate overnight.

Make the Glaze: In a small bowl, combine the oyster sauce, soy sauce, honey, water and annatto oil. Set it aside.

Form the Sausages: Soak 15 wooden skewers in a tray of water for at least 30 minutes. If you prefer, you can also form sausages without using skewers, or make meatballs. This will yield 12 to 15 sausages.

Remove the pork paste from the fridge 1 hour before cooking. Have ready a bowl of water to wet your hands and wear food-safe plastic gloves. Spread the paste on a tray and flatten it into a 1-inch (2.5-cm)-thick rectangle. Use a spatula to precut vertical lines 1 inch (2.5 cm) apart and form each strip into a 5-inch (13-cm)-long sausage around each wooden skewer, leaving at least an inch (2.5 cm) uncovered at one end so you can hold the skewer.

Panfry the Sausages: Brush the glaze on the pork. In a large skillet, heat the oil over medium-high heat. You will be cooking the skewers in two batches—don't overcrowd the pan, or the meat will steam instead of brown. Cook the first batch for about 8 minutes, rotating them halfway through that time. Brush on more of the glaze, then cook for 2 minutes. Add 1 tablespoon (15 ml) of water to deglaze the pan if the glaze begins to burn. In between batches, add water and wipe down the pan if needed. Cook the second batch of skewers.

Serve: Enjoy the sausages with a side of rice vermicelli noodles, lettuce, perilla leaves and peanut sauce.

Caramelized Ground Pork Bowl (Thịt Băm)

This 20-minute meal is my go-to recipe when I need to get dinner on the table ASAP. The caramelized bits of ground pork and onion provide textural crispy bits of sweet and savory. The best part is that this dish bursts with flavors from simple ingredients such as fish sauce, sugar, garlic and onion. Alternatively, you can substitute ground chicken, turkey or beef for the pork.

Yield: 2 to 3 servings

2 tbsp (30 ml) neutral cooking oil

6 cloves garlic, minced

1 bird's eye chile, sliced and seeded (optional)

½ large yellow onion, chopped

1 lb (455 g) ground pork

2 tbsp (30 ml) fish sauce

3 tbsp (45 g) light or dark brown sugar

For Serving

Cooked rice

Lettuce, sliced

Pickled Carrots and Daikon (page 182)

Panfry the Pork: In a large skillet, heat the oil over medium-high heat and sauté the garlic and bird's eye chile for 30 seconds before adding the chopped onion. Cook until the onion is softened and starts caramelizing, about 4 minutes. Add the ground pork and break it up into little pieces. Cook until it is almost no longer pink, 3 to 4 minutes. Mix in the fish sauce and brown sugar. Cook undisturbed for 3 minutes. Mix well, then cook undisturbed for 2 minutes. Repeat to mix and then cook undisturbed for 1 minute at a time, until the pork is caramelized and has some crunchy bits.

Serve: Plate the ground pork over rice and serve with lettuce, plus pickled carrots and daikon. Or serve as lettuce wraps.

Fried Tofu with Fermented Shrimp Paste Sauce
(Bún Đậu Mắm Tôm)

This signature dish of Hanoi is known for its pungent, funky fermented shrimp sauce that brings together the components of fried tofu, slices of pork, rice vermicelli and herbs. Look for fermented shrimp paste (Mắm Tôm) in a glass jar located in the condiments section of your local Asian market. If this potent sauce isn't for you, replace it with Nước Chấm (page 178) or Peanut Sauce (page 183). In some regions, the rice vermicelli is cooked, then pressed into a baking dish and cut into 1-inch (2.5-cm) blocks after it has cooled, for a textural twist.

Similar to the way I've connected to my Vietnamese roots, I've noticed Mom connecting to Northern dishes more recently. Hanoi food reminds her of Grandma's hometown before they fled down South to Saigon when the country was divided in 1954.

Yield: 2 to 4 servings

Noodles

1 lb (455 g) dried rice vermicelli noodles

Pork Belly

1½ lb (680 g) pork belly

1 tbsp (18 g) salt

1 (½" [1.3-cm]) knob fresh ginger, sliced

Panfried Tofu

1 (1-lb [455-g]) block firm tofu

½ cup (120 ml) neutral cooking oil, for panfrying

Fermented Shrimp Paste Sauce (Mắm Tôm)

3 tbsp (45 g) fermented shrimp paste

2 tbsp (26 g) sugar

2 tbsp (30 ml) water

Juice of 1 lime

3 cloves garlic, minced

1 tbsp (15 ml) chili sauce

For Serving

Fresh mint, perilla leaves, fish mint leaves

Cook the Noodles: Follow the package instructions to cook the noodles. Place the cooked noodles in a baking dish, piled 1 inch (2.5 cm) high. Cover with plastic wrap and lay another baking dish on top to press the noodles down. Leave them for 30 minutes to bind together. Remove the plastic wrap and place a plate on top of the baking dish. Flip the dish over to release the noodle block, then cut into 1-inch (2.5-cm) cubes.

Boil the Pork: In a large pot, combine the pork belly, salt, ginger and enough water to submerge the pork. Over medium-high heat, bring the liquid to a boil. Cover, lower the heat to medium-low and simmer for 40 minutes, or until tender. Drain and discard the liquid. Rinse the pork belly under cold water, let it rest for 10 minutes, then slice into thin pieces.

Panfry the Tofu: Press down on the block of tofu with a paper towel or cheesecloth, and pat dry. Cut the tofu into 2 x 1–inch (5 x 2.5-cm), ½-inch (1.3-cm)–thick rectangles and pat them dry again. In a large skillet, heat the oil over medium-high heat and fry the tofu in a single layer. Cook the tofu undisturbed for about 4 minutes, then flip and cook for 4 minutes, until golden brown all around.

Make the Fermented Shrimp Paste Sauce: In a small bowl, combine the fermented shrimp paste, sugar, water, lime juice, garlic and chili sauce. Adjust to taste by adding more water, salt, lime juice or sugar.

Serve: On a platter, arrange the fried tofu, slices of pork belly, noodles, herbs and fermented shrimp paste sauce to enjoy family style.

Vegan Fried Tofu with Peanut Dressing
(Đậu Hũ Chiên)

These deep-fried tofu puffs are crispy on the outside and soft and spongy on the inside. Frying the tofu keeps it from falling apart, which also makes it a great vegan option for replacing meat. This recipe is dedicated to my late uncle, Bác Anh, who went vegetarian in his recent years. Somewhat of a genius, Mom's brother left for Germany on a college scholarship when she was 10 years old. When the Vietnam War ended, Mom's family didn't think they could reach him due to the circumstances. Nearly 30 years later, our uncle knocked on our door. There was no better way to make up for lost time than with Mom's cooking. She would prepare a Vietnamese vegetarian feast when he visited. Using fried tofu, she re-created vermicelli bowls, soups, braises, stir-fries and Bánh with its substantive texture.

Yield: 4 servings

Fried Tofu Puffs

2 lb (908 g) firm tofu

2 cups (475 ml) neutral cooking oil

Salt, to taste

Peanut Dressing

1 tbsp (15 ml) neutral cooking oil

2 cloves garlic, minced

¼ cup (64 g) peanut butter

¼ cup (60 ml) hoisin sauce

1¼ cups (295 ml) water

Juice of 1 lime

2 tbsp (36 g) chili garlic sauce

¼ cup (35 g) roasted crushed peanuts (optional)

For Serving

1 lb (455 g) dried rice vermicelli noodles, cooked

Fresh cilantro, Vietnamese coriander, perilla leaves

Pickled Carrots and Daikon (page 182)

Prepare the Tofu: Pat the tofu dry and cut it into 9 or 18 cubes. The larger blocks of tofu puff up more, but 18 is also a good size and offers more bites, so the size is up to you.

Fry the Tofu: In a medium-sized, deep pot, heat the oil to 375°F (190°C). Fry the tofu in batches, lowering the tofu into the oil with a spider colander or strainer so it doesn't splash. Use a wooden chopstick to swirl the oil for the first 2 minutes to keep the tofu pieces from sticking to one another.

Cook the tofu until it puffs up and turns an even golden brown, 8 to 10 minutes. Adjust the heat as necessary. Be patient and resist turning up the heat to fry the tofu faster. It needs time to cook out the excess water inside before it can puff up. Also, be careful not to overcook the tofu, or it will be dry inside. Transfer the fried tofu to a cooling rack or a paper towel–lined plate to remove the excess oil. Sprinkle with a pinch of salt.

Make the Peanut Dressing: In a small saucepan, heat the oil over medium heat and sauté the garlic for 1 minute. Add the peanut butter, hoisin sauce and water. Mix until incorporated and smooth. Add the lime juice, chili garlic sauce and crushed peanuts.

Serve: Plate the fried tofu over rice vermicelli noodles and the herbs. Top with pickled carrots and daikon, and drizzle with the peanut sauce.

Vietnamese Grilled Pork Chops and Broken Rice
(Cơm Tấm Sườn Nướng)

"Cơm Tấm" refers to "broken rice" plates, which are a Southern specialty. These originated during economic hardships and food shortages. Farmers didn't have enough rice to sell due to poor harvest conditions. Fragments of rice left over from the milling process couldn't be sold, so they cooked with the "broken" rice. In the mid-'90s, Vietnam became one of the world's largest exporters of rice, with an economic resurgence making broken rice dishes widely available. Today, the Mekong Delta and the Red River Delta, known as Vietnam's two "rice baskets," are responsible for the country's rice cultivation. Saigon adapted Cơm Tấm with bold variations to appeal to the masses. Restaurants now serve plates with up to 15 item combinations, but grilled pork chops are almost always the main attraction.

Yield: 6 servings

2 to 3 lb (905 g to 1.4 kg) pork chops (about 6 thick pork chops)

¼ cup (17 g) finely minced lemongrass

2 shallots, minced

1 head garlic, minced

3 tbsp (45 ml) fish sauce

1 tsp dark soy sauce

¼ cup (60 g) light or dark brown sugar

1 tbsp (15 ml) honey

3 tbsp (45 ml) neutral oil, divided, if panfrying, or 1 tbsp (15 ml) if air frying

Cooking oil spray, if air frying

For Serving

Cooked jasmine rice or broken rice

Scallion Oil (page 180)

Pickled Carrots and Daikon (page 182) or Pickled Cabbage and Carrots (page 182)

Nước Chấm (page 178)

Vietnamese Egg Meatloaf (page 43, optional)

Marinate the Pork: Rinse the pork under cold water to remove any loose bone fragments. Pat dry. In a large bowl, coat the pork chops with the lemongrass, shallots, garlic, fish sauce, dark soy sauce, brown sugar, honey and 1 tablespoon (15 ml) of the oil. Cover and marinate in the fridge for at least 6 hours, ideally overnight for best results.

Panfry Method: In a large skillet, heat 1 tablespoon (15 ml) of oil over high heat. You will be cooking the pork in two batches—don't overcrowd the pan, or the meat will steam instead of brown. Brown half of the pork for 3 to 4 minutes per side, depending on thickness. Panfry over high heat to get a sear on the pork and flip it over. Add a few drops of water, swirl the pan around to prevent the marinade from burning and continue cooking. Transfer the pork to a plate. Add an additional 1 tablespoon (15ml) of oil and cook the second batch of pork.

Air Fryer Method: Preheat an air fryer to 380°F (193°C) for 10 minutes. Spray with cooking oil and add the pork chops. Do not overcrowd the tray or it will steam instead of brown. The temperature and timing will depend on the thickness of the pork chops. For ½-inch (1.3-cm)–thick pork chops, air fry at 380°F (193°C) for 7 minutes on each side. For thinner pork chops, air fry at 375°F (190°C) for 7 minutes on each side. The internal temperature should reach 145°F (64°C).

Serve: Plate the pork chops whole over cooked rice and top with scallion oil and pickled vegetables, with a side of Nước Chấm. Optionally, add a slice of Vietnamese egg meatloaf.

Pro Tip: The dish is so popular that many choose to break full-grain rice for its unique texture that absorbs flavor so well. To do this, rinse the uncooked rice grains and soak them in cold water for an hour. Drain the water and rub the rice through your fingers to manually break the grains before cooking. You can also buy broken rice grains.

Vietnamese Egg Meatloaf (Chả Trứng)

This delicious, unassuming meatloaf was a regular for my childhood dinners as an entrée in itself. It is fluffy and spongy, with various textures from the noodles and mushrooms. Now, I always order it with my broken rice dish at Vietnamese restaurants, but this recipe is simple and affordable to make on a weeknight. Mom would supplement dinner with a pot of Canh (soup) to fill us up and provide extra nutrients. Her soup didn't have a recipe. It consisted of chicken broth, water and her choice of vegetables, seasoned with a dash of fish sauce and black pepper.

Yield: 6 servings

1 (2-oz [55-g]) bundle dried mung bean thread noodles

½ cup (10 g) dried wood ear mushrooms

8 oz (225 g) ground pork

½ medium-sized yellow onion, chopped

3 cloves garlic, minced

1 tbsp (15 ml) fish sauce

1 tsp sugar

1 tsp chicken bouillon powder

1 tsp salt

½ tsp freshly ground black pepper

6 large eggs, divided

2 tsp (10 ml) Annatto Oil (page 181, optional)

Neutral cooking oil, for brushing onto aluminum foil (optional)

For Serving:

Cooked rice

Nước Chấm (page 178)

Make the Filling: In a small bowl of water, soak the dried mung bean noodles and dried wood ear mushrooms for about 20 minutes, or until softened. Drain, pat dry and use scissors to cut the noodles and mushrooms into ⅜-inch (1-cm) pieces.

In a large bowl, combine the pork, noodles, mushrooms, onion, garlic, fish sauce, sugar, chicken bouillon powder, salt and pepper. Crack four of the eggs into the mixture. Into two separate small bowls, separate the remaining two eggs: whites in one bowl, yolks in the other. Add the whites to the meatloaf mixture and mix well. To the yolks in their separate bowl, add the annatto oil if you're looking to achieve a red-orange hue versus a golden yellow layer on top. Set aside for later.

Prepare the Baking Dish: Line an 8-inch (20-cm) round baking dish or cake pan with parchment paper or aluminum foil, ensuring the paper or foil extends 1 inch (2.5 cm) higher than the dish's edges all around. This will make it easier to remove the meatloaf from the dish after cooking. If using foil, brush it with oil. Spread the meatloaf in an even layer. The meatloaf should be about 1½ inches (4 cm) thick.

Steam: Prepare a steamer with water according to the manufacturer's directions. If you don't have a steamer, see page 19 for tips on preparing a makeshift steamer.

Bring the water to a gentle rolling boil over medium-high heat. Place the baking dish on the steamer tray and put it in the steamer. Cover and steam for 25 minutes. Brush an even layer of the yolk on top, cover, then steam for 5 minutes. The center should be firm but bouncy. The internal temperature of ground pork should reach 160°F (71°C). Remove from the steamer. Let cool for 15 minutes before slicing, or the meatloaf will fall apart. The cooking time depends on the steamer tray or the thickness of the meatloaf.

Serve: Enjoy this meatloaf with rice and Nước Chấm. Or serve it as an accompaniment to Vietnamese Grilled Pork Chops and Broken Rice (page 40).

Home Away from Home

Soups, Braises and Stews

For my parents, Phở feels like the comfort of home. To me, Phở feels like an undeniable connection to my heritage. When I eat a bowl, I'm reminded of another part of my identity. Over the years, my exposure to the multiplicity of soups and cuisine beyond Phở has shown me that there is much more to discover about Vietnam and my culture. Each soup reveals its own story about the geography, people and history behind it.

In the Northern region, neighboring China, you'll find soups with a clear, light but flavorful broth that is unadulterated by excess condiments. Such soups as Phở and Vietnamese Crab Noodle Soup (Bún Riêu Cua, page 51) have a "less is more" approach to toppings and condiments. Flavors are light and balanced to showcase the natural taste of the ingredients. The colder climate limits the availability of herbs and spices, so you'll find less use of herbs, and the use of black pepper instead of chile. The region also prides itself on traditional dishes that reflect the origin of Vietnam before it expanded its territory.

By the eighteenth century, Vietnam's dynasties conquered the central region from the Cham people and a portion of the Khmer Empire in the South, forming the country's dragonlike shape. In the Central region, you'll find bold flavors to represent the former ancient royal court. The Spicy Beef Noodle Soup (Bún Bò Huế, page 57), and Quảng-Style Turmeric Noodle Soup (Mì Quảng, page 61) are substantial and fit for the emperor. The warmer climate is ideal for growing chiles, so you'll find a preference for hot and spicy flavors. And with access to a long coastline, seafood is preserved by making fermented shrimp and anchovy pastes known as Mắm in Vietnamese, which adds a pungent kick.

In the Southern region, the soups are on the sweeter side and are garnished with a "more is more" approach to toppings and condiments. The warmer climate, fertile soil and access to the Mekong Delta support a thriving agriculture to grow produce, livestock and seafood. Cambodian Phnom Penh Noodle Soup (Hủ Tiếu Nam Vang, page 63), Tapioca Noodle Soup with Crab (Bánh Canh Cua, page 67) and Sour Seafood Soup (Canh Chua, page 68) are some popular soups that showcase the fresh seafood from the region.

With my parents from the North (Hà Nội), Central (Huế), and South (Sài Gòn) and my in-laws from the Southern Central Coast (Nha Trang), I'm fortunate to have tasted and learned different cooking styles and preferences. Every family has its own version of soups, braises and stews. I hope you enjoy ours and put your own spin on them. A soup, braise or stew slowly simmers and cooks at its own pace. It goes through a process that can't be rushed and forces you to slow down to enjoy the ride. Although these recipes take time, the steps are simple. Once you understand the concepts, you'll be able to make these dishes by memory.

Mastering Soups

Behind every good slurp is a solid bone broth achieved by following these general guidelines. Simmering bones, aromatics and vegetables in a pot of water extracts and harmonizes the ingredients.

1. Use Bones
Bags of beef and pork bones are available at an Asian market or butcher shop. Look for bones or for meat that has bones with a lot of connective tissue and cartilage because they are collagen-rich. Examples include whole chicken, chicken feet or wings; pork hocks, ribs and knuckles; and beef bone marrow, oxtail, bone-in shank and knuckles. When these are cooked for a long time, the structural proteins of the collagen in the bones and connective tissue breaks down into the liquid, providing that silky texture. When the broth cools, the proteins form a gelatinous texture the next day. The gelatin will liquefy when reheated, giving the broth body and depth of flavor. Many factors determine how much your broth will gel, including the quality and type of bones used, the ratio of bones to water, cooking temperatures and length of simmering time, which can take up to 12 hours.

2. Parboil the Meat and Bones to Remove the Scum
For a meat-based broth, it starts with parboiling, a method that involves an initial boil followed by a cold rinse. When the meat and bones are cooked, the excess blood vessels release into the water and rise to the top. These impurities that collect in the form of foam are referred to as scum. By parboiling, you can remove the scum before making the soup, resulting in a cleaner and clearer broth. If you skip this step, alternatively you can skim the broth while it is cooking, but it can be more time consuming and less thorough.

3. Char and Toast the Aromatics
Charring the onion and ginger will release a smoky depth of flavor, while cooking it until it is slightly softened on the inside will add sweetness to soups like Phở. Toasting the seasonings, spices and aromatics releases their natural oils and aroma. Similarly, charring the dried squid or dried shrimp for the pork and seafood soups will develop a smoky umami flavor if you have time. Each of these steps adds another layer of flavor.

4. Slowly Simmer
Simmering beef, pork, chicken or fish bones slowly will extract the collagen, providing a nutrient and flavor-rich broth. It also helps the flavors meld together, as opposed to boiling at a high temperature, which instead concentrates and reduces the liquid and cooks the outside of the meat too fast. However, before simmering, bring the liquid to a boil so it is hot enough to extract the collagen from the bones. If using a lid, tilt it to vent and keep a close eye on it so that the liquid does not boil over. As soon as it starts to boil, cover, lower the heat to low and simmer to maintain the temperature. The broth should have small bubbles that steadily rise to the top and pop. Lower the heat further if there are rapid bubbles, which will cause the broth to get cloudy because of all the jostling around in the water. On the other hand, increase the heat just a little if there are barely any bubbles, because we need some movement in the water to marry the flavors.

Cooking times: The amount of time listed in the soup recipes is the minimum for simmering to result in a flavorful broth. Of course, the broth will be richer the longer the bones are simmered, if you have time. If you plan to simmer the bones for 6 to 12 hours, don't add in the aromatics until the final 3 hours, or the flavors of the aromatics will mellow out.

Simmering also tenderizes the meat and allows for even cooking. For a whole chicken (3 to 5 pounds [1.4 to 2.3 kg]), simmer for 30 minutes to 1½ hours, depending on its size. For beef roasts (chuck, brisket, shank), simmer for 2 to 3 hours. For pork loin or hocks, simmer for 1 hour, and for pork ribs, about 2½ hours.

5. Strain the Broth and Skim the Oil

Discard the solids (aromatics) and strain the broth to ensure it is clear. You can also pour the broth through a fine strainer directly into a serving bowl over the prepared noodles. Before serving, skim the oil with a spoon, use a fat separator or refrigerate the broth and remove the solidified block of fat the next day. Although some oil can add flavor, too much oil can detract from the taste.

6. Season and Adjust to Taste

Adjusting to taste at the end or along the way is a common practice in a Vietnamese kitchen. For Mom, a little fish sauce is introduced at the beginning and the additional fish sauce is added toward the end, to taste. This is because the soup is simmering for a long period of time. After tasting the flavors melded together, you can decide how much to add; all the flavor won't be wasted on the discarded solids and the smell of fish sauce won't be permeating the air all day. These recipes don't require it, but adding a pinch of MSG can add an extra edge.

7. Modify As Needed

Don't be discouraged by a recipe for lack of time or access to ingredients. If you aren't able to find bones, omit them and follow the same process; the broth will be thinner and less rich, but still delicious. Try to find a cut with bones or use store-bought stock and fortify it with aromatics or soup bases, such as from the brand Quốc Việt Foods®, which also has vegan options!

Beef Phở Rice Noodle Soup (Phở Bò)

Vietnam's national dish was birthed in the North during the 1880s. Although its exact origin is unclear, it is likely that Phở has influence from Chinese and French cooking. Rice noodles and spices were imported from China, while the use of beef for consumption was introduced by the French. However, it was the ingenious way the dish was put together by the Vietnamese cooks that truly represents the resilience of the country, using leftover beef bones to create something beautiful during difficult times.

After the end of French colonialism and the First Indochina War, Vietnam was divided in 1954 into the North and South. Over 1 million people fled south, bringing with them their love of Phở where it grew increasingly popular and was adapted to regional tastes. Northern Phở is left pure with only the addition of green onion, chiles and lime, whereas Southern Phở is sweeter and adorned with bean sprouts, herbs, hoisin sauce and Sriracha. Optionally, add the precooked meatballs labeled "Bò Viên," located in the refrigerated aisle of Vietnamese markets.

Yield: 6 servings

Broth

3 lb (1.4 kg) boneless beef chuck roast or brisket

2 to 3 lb (905 g to 1.4 kg) beef bones

2 tbsp (36 g) salt, divided

4½ qt (18 cups [4 L]) water, for broth

3 tbsp (45 ml) fish sauce, plus more to taste

1 (1½" [4-cm], 50-g) piece yellow rock sugar, or 1 tbsp (13 g) granulated sugar

Aromatics

2 large yellow onions, peeled and cut in half

1 (2" [5-cm]) knob fresh ginger, peeled and cut in half

1 to 2 tbsp (15 to 30 ml) neutral cooking oil (optional)

Spices

3 cinnamon sticks

2 tbsp (10 g) coriander seeds

1 tbsp (6 g) fennel seeds

1 tsp whole cloves

5 star anise

Parboil the Beef Roast and Bones: In an 8-quart (8-L) or larger stockpot, combine the beef roast and bones with enough water to cover without boiling over. Add ½ tablespoon (9 g) of salt and bring the liquid to a boil on high heat, uncovered. This may take up to 20 minutes. Once boiling, cook for 5 minutes and drain. Discard the liquid and rinse the beef and bones under cold water to remove the impurities. Set aside in a large bowl. Clean the stockpot and return the beef roast and bones back to it.

Char the Aromatics: Broil the onions and ginger on the top rack of your oven for 15 minutes or until charred. Flip, and char the other side for 10 minutes. Alternatively, char in a medium-sized skillet with 1 to 2 tablespoons (15 to 30 ml) of oil over medium-high heat for about 10 minutes, flipping halfway through.

Toast the Spices: In a small skillet, dry toast the cinnamon sticks, coriander seeds, fennel seeds, whole cloves and star anise over medium heat for 1 to 2 minutes to release their aroma. Transfer them to a stainless-steel spice infuser or bag, or add directly to the pot and strain out later.

Make the Broth: To the stockpot, add the fresh water, charred onions, ginger, toasted spice mixture, 1½ tablespoons (27 g) of salt, fish sauce and rock sugar. Bring the liquid to a boil, uncovered, over high heat. Lower the heat to low, cover and simmer for 2 to 3 hours, or until the beef is tender. Transfer the beef to a bowl and set aside.

Cover and simmer the broth for 2 hours. Discard the solids. Strain the broth into another pot, or use a strainer to remove any small bits. Skim off the oil and season the broth with additional fish sauce, rock sugar or water to taste.

When the beef has cooled completely, trim the beef fat and slice the roast.

(continued)

For Serving

1 lb (455 g) store-bought Vietnamese beef meatballs, cut in half (optional)

1½ lb (680 g) dried or 2 lb (905 g) fresh small flat rice noodles, cooked

8 oz (225 g) beef eye round or "hot pot beef," sliced thinly

1 large yellow onion, thinly sliced

4 green onions, sliced

Fresh culantro, Thai basil, cilantro, mint, sliced jalapeño

12 oz (340 g) mung bean sprouts

2 limes, cut into wedges

Sriracha

Hoisin sauce

Serve: Reheat the prepared Vietnamese beef meatballs in the broth for 5 minutes just before serving. To each large serving bowl, add the noodles and slices of roast and meatballs. Place the raw slices of beef eye round in the bowl; the meat will cook once the piping hot broth is poured on top. Ladle in 2½ cups (590 ml) of the hot broth. Top with sliced onion, green onion, herbs, mung bean sprouts and a lime wedge. Keep the Sriracha and hoisin sauce bottles on the table.

Vietnamese Crab Noodle Soup (Bún Riêu Cua)

This soup is known for its signature meatballs, or Riêu, made from a mixture of crabmeat, ground pork and egg bathed in a crab paste, tomato and meat-based broth. This soup originated in the Northern Red River Delta. Traditionally, freshwater paddy crabs are ground into a paste and the strained liquid is the broth base, but we're using store-bought crab paste. The following is my mother-in-law's recipe, slightly modified. Shelling the freshly steamed crabs is a laborious task that my father-in-law undertakes as her sous chef. However, we're using lump crabmeat to make life easier. The crab paste is often labeled "Gạch Cua Xào Dầu Ăn" (crab paste with bean oil); alternatively, you can use the can labeled "Minced Crab in Spices," found in Asian markets.

Yield: 6 servings (25 to 30 meatballs)

Crab and Pork Meatballs

¼ cup (20 g) dried scallops or dried shrimp (optional)

1 lb (455 g) ground pork

8 oz (225 g) lump crabmeat, cooked

2 oz (55 g) crab paste with bean oil, or 3 oz (85 g) canned minced crab in spices

1½ tbsp (23 ml) fish sauce

⅛ tsp salt

½ tsp freshly ground black pepper

4 large eggs

Broth

3½ qt (14 cups [3 L]) water, for broth

1½ tbsp (9 g) chicken bouillon powder

2½ tbsp (38 ml) fish sauce, plus more to taste

1 (1½" [4-cm], 50-g) piece yellow rock sugar, or 1 tbsp (13 g) granulated sugar

1 tbsp (15 ml) neutral cooking oil

1 large yellow onion, sliced

2 large shallots, sliced

2 oz (55 g) crab paste with bean oil, or 3 oz (85 g) canned minced crab in spices, plus more to taste

4 Roma tomatoes, quartered

1 lb (455 g) shrimp, peeled and deveined

15 pieces Fried Tofu Puffs (page 39 or store-bought, optional)

Prepare the Crab and Pork Meatballs: If using, soak the dried scallops or dried shrimp in a bowl of cold water for 20 minutes, or until softened. Drain and discard the liquid. If using shrimp, grind it in a food processor. If using scallops, pull it apart with your fingers into shreds. In a large bowl, gently combine the scallops or shrimp, ground pork, crabmeat, crab paste, fish sauce, salt, pepper and eggs. Do not overmix. The mixture should be light (not dense) with some lumps of crabmeat still intact. Cover and refrigerate for at least 15 minutes.

Make the Broth: In an 8-quart (8-L) stockpot, combine the water, chicken bouillon powder, fish sauce and rock sugar, and heat, covered, over medium heat. In a large skillet, heat the oil over medium-high heat and cook the onion and shallots until softened, about 3 minutes. Add the crab paste and tomatoes to the onion mixture. Sauté for 2 minutes, or until heated through. Transfer the mixture to the stockpot. Mix 1 cup (240 ml) of the broth into the skillet to deglaze the caramelized bits of sauce and pour back into the pot. Cover and increase the heat to medium-high. Once the broth starts to boil, taste it. Add more water, crab paste, fish sauce and/or rock sugar, if needed.

Cook the Meatballs and Shrimp: Use a large spoon to scoop 1 to 2 tablespoons (15 to 28 g) of the meatball mixture and loosely form it into a ball. The balls should be fluffy and airy inside when cooked. Quickly lower them in the pot of broth. The meatballs are cooked when they float to the top, 3 to 4 minutes.

Turn off the heat. Use a strainer to lower the shrimp into the pot to cook for 2 to 3 minutes, then transfer them to a bowl once the shrimp curls into a C shape; if they curl into an O shape, they are overcooked. Mix the fried tofu puffs into the pot to heat through and turn the heat back on to medium to warm the broth.

(continued)

For Serving

2 lb (905 g) dried rice vermicelli noodles, cooked

6 green onions, sliced

Fresh cilantro, mint, perilla leaves or Thai basil

1 lb (455 g) mung bean sprouts

2 limes, cut into wedges

Jarred fermented shrimp paste

Serve: To each large serving bowl, add the rice vermicelli noodles, shrimp, meatballs and onion mixture. Ladle in 2 cups (475 ml) of hot broth. Top with green onion, cilantro, mint, perilla leaves, mung bean sprouts and a lime wedge. Keep the jar of fermented shrimp paste at the table.

Chicken Phở Rice Noodle Soup (Phở Gà)

Phở Gà was first created in 1939, when the government limited the supply of beef for consumption. The sale of beef was forbidden on Mondays and Fridays, and chicken Phở was born to satisfy cravings. Although it was first met with resistance, its taste proved it deserved its own lane of recognition. If done right, you'll end up with tender pieces of chicken and a flavor-rich but light broth. While Phở can be intimidating, the steps are relatively easy once you get the hang of them. Using free-range, cage-free chicken, known as "walking chicken" (Gà Đi Bộ), gives the meat chewiness, a preferred Vietnamese texture. However, it isn't required.

Yield: 6 servings

Broth

1 (3- to 5-lb [1.4- to 2.3-kg]) whole chicken, giblets removed

2 tbsp (36 g) salt, divided

4½ qt (18 cups [4 L]) water, for broth

3 tbsp (45 ml) fish sauce, plus more to taste

1 (1½" [4-cm], 50-g) piece yellow rock sugar, or 1 tbsp (13 g) granulated sugar

Aromatics

2 large yellow onions, peeled and cut in half

1 (2" [5-cm]) knob fresh ginger, peeled and cut in half

1 to 2 tbsp (15 to 30 ml) neutral cooking oil (optional)

Spices

3 cinnamon sticks

2 tbsp (10 g) coriander seeds

1 tbsp (6 g) fennel seeds

5 star anise

1½ tsp (3 g) whole cloves

Parboil the Chicken: In an 8-quart (8-L) or larger stockpot, combine the chicken and ½ tablespoon (9 g) of salt. Make sure the pot is large enough to add enough water to submerge the chicken by 2 inches (5 cm) without boiling over. Bring the liquid to a boil, uncovered, over high heat. This may take up to 20 minutes. Once boiling, cook for 5 minutes. Discard the liquid and gently rinse the chicken and its cavity with cold water. Set aside in a large bowl. Clean the stockpot and return the chicken to it.

Char the Aromatics: Broil the onions and ginger on the top rack of your oven for 15 minutes, or until charred. Flip, and char the other side for 10 minutes. Alternatively, char in a medium-sized skillet with 1 to 2 tablespoons (15 to 30 ml) of oil over medium-high heat for about 10 minutes, flipping halfway through.

Toast the Spices: In a small skillet, dry toast the cinnamon sticks, coriander seeds, fennel seeds, star anise and whole cloves in a pan over medium heat for 1 to 2 minutes to release their aroma. Transfer them to a stainless-steel spice infuser or bag, or add directly to the pot and strain out later.

Make the Broth: To the stockpot, add the fresh water, onions, ginger, toasted spice mixture, remaining 1½ tablespoons (27 g) of salt, fish sauce and rock sugar. Bring the liquid to a boil, uncovered, over high heat. Lower the heat to low, cover and simmer until the chicken is cooked. Depending on the size of the chicken, this can take from 30 minutes to 1½ hours. To test for doneness, poke the deepest part of the breast with a chopstick—the juices should run clear, and for a safe internal temperature it should reach 165°F (73°C). Use tongs to transfer the chicken to an ice bath for a minute. Drain and let cool, about 15 minutes, before shredding or slicing.

Return the carcass to the pot, cover and simmer over low heat for 1 to 2 hours. Remove the solids. Strain the broth into another pot or use a strainer to remove any small bits. Skim off the oil and season the broth with additional fish sauce, rock sugar or water, to taste.

(continued)

For Serving

1½ lb (680 g) dried or 2 lb (905 g) fresh small flat rice noodles, cooked

1 large yellow onion, sliced thinly

4 green onions, sliced

Fresh culantro, Thai basil, cilantro, mint, sliced jalapeño

12 oz (340 g) mung bean sprouts

2 limes, cut into wedges

Sriracha

Hoisin sauce

Serve: To each large serving bowl, add the noodles and pieces of chicken. Ladle in 2½ cups (590 ml) of hot broth. Top with the onion, green onion, culantro, cilantro, mint, jalapeño, mung bean sprouts and a lime wedge. Keep the Sriracha and hoisin sauce bottles on the table.

Notes: Parboiling results in the clearest broth. If you prefer to skip this step, rub salt on the chicken and rinse it carefully under cold water to clean it. Place the chicken in the pot and follow the instructions for "Make the Broth." Skim the scum throughout the cooking process.

Spicy Beef Noodle Soup (Bún Bò Huế)

In her early twenties, my oldest sister would often request this fiery soup, which reflected her personality and bold taste. The broth is made from beef bones and cuts of beef and pork meat, simmered for hours with lemongrass as the star aromatic. The soup's brimming red hue comes from the Sate Chili Oil (page 181), packed with umami flavor. The funk of shrimp paste makes this soup flavor-forward. The noodles, unlike other "Bún" vermicelli, are much larger and robust.

To make this soup, plan ahead. Make the Sate Chili Oil in advance or purchase it. Beef shank has a lot of tendons intertwined in the meat. Tie kitchen twine around it so that it cooks evenly and is easy to cut later. If you aren't a fan of tendons, opt for a meaty chuck roast or brisket. If you can't find lemongrass, omit it. The steamed pork meatloaf can be found at a Vietnamese market in the refrigerated section.

Yield: 6 servings

Broth

3 lb (1.4 kg) boneless beef chuck roast, shank or brisket

1½ lb (680 g) boneless pork leg, shank or sliced hocks

2 to 3 lb (908 g to 1.4 kg) beef bones, or beef with bones

2 tbsp (36 g) salt, divided, plus more to taste

4½ qt (18 cups [4 L]) water, for broth

3 lemongrass stalks, center-cut pieces cut into 3" (7.5-cm) lengths, bruised

3 tbsp (45 ml) fish sauce, plus more to taste

1½ tsp (3 g) beef bouillon powder

1 (1" [2.5-cm], 30-g) piece yellow rock sugar, or 1½ tsp (7 g) granulated sugar

2 tbsp (14 g) paprika, or (7 g) red pepper flakes

Aromatics

1 large yellow onion

1 (2" [5-cm]) knob fresh ginger, cut into pieces

1 to 2 tbsp (15 to 30 ml) neutral cooking oil (optional)

½ cup (120 ml) Sate Chili Oil (page 181 or store-bought), divided

Parboil the Beef, Pork and Bones: In a large stockpot, combine the beef, pork and bones with enough water to cover. Add ½ tablespoon (9 g) of salt and bring the liquid to a boil, uncovered, over high heat so the liquid doesn't boil over. This may take up to 20 minutes. Once boiling, cook for 5 minutes. Discard the liquid and rinse the beef, pork and bones under cold water to remove the impurities. Set aside in a large bowl. Clean the stockpot and return the beef, pork and bones to it.

Char the Aromatics: Broil the onion and ginger on the top rack of your oven for 15 minutes, or until charred. Alternatively, char in a skillet with 1 to 2 tablespoons (15 to 30 ml) of oil over medium to medium-high heat for about 10 minutes, flipping halfway through.

Make the Broth: To the stockpot, add the fresh water, lemongrass, onion, ginger, 1½ tablespoons (27 g) of salt, fish sauce, beef bouillon powder, rock sugar and paprika. Bring the liquid to a boil, uncovered, over high heat. Lower the heat to low, cover and simmer until the pork is tender, about 1½ hours. Transfer the pork to a bowl.

Continue to simmer the broth until the beef is tender (about 45 minutes for chuck roast, or up to 1½ hours for brisket or shank). It will be easier to slice the beef and pork against the grain once the meat has cooled completely. Slice, sprinkle with salt to taste and set aside in a bowl.

Discard the solids from the broth and skim off the oil. Add ¼ cup (60 ml) of the sate chili oil. Taste and adjust with fish sauce, rock sugar or water.

(continued)

For Serving

28 oz (800 g) dried Bún Bò Huế noodles or thick vermicelli rice noodles, cooked

8 oz (225 g) store-bought Vietnamese steamed pork meatloaf, sliced (optional)

½ head cabbage, sliced (about 1 lb [455 g] sliced)

1 onion, sliced thinly

½ cup (30 g) Fried Shallots (page 180)

Fresh mint, cilantro, sliced green onion, Thai basil

12 oz (340 g) mung bean sprouts

3 limes, quartered

Jarred fermented shrimp paste

Serve: To each large serving bowl, add the noodles topped with layers of beef, pork and steamed pork meatloaf (if using). Ladle in 2 cups (475 ml) of the piping hot broth. Top with cabbage, onion, fried shallots, mint, cilantro, sliced green onion, Thai basil, mung bean sprouts and a lime wedge. Leave the remaining ¼ cup (60 ml) of sate chili oil and the jar of fermented shrimp paste at the table.

Quảng-Style Turmeric Noodle Soup (Mì Quảng)

This vibrant, golden yellow noodle soup originates from the Quảng Nam province in the Central region. The noodles lay on a bed of greens adorned with sautéed pork, shrimp, pineapple and a variety of toppings. Unlike most Vietnamese soups, there is usually just enough broth to wet the noodles, but our family likes to add more broth. The bone broth can be chicken, pork, beef or even seafood. My best friend's family invited me to dinner at a restaurant that specializes in Mì Quảng. Mom upped the game by making her own special version.

Yield: 6 servings

Broth

3 lb (1.4 kg) pork ribs

1½ tbsp (27 g) salt, divided

2 tbsp (30 ml) neutral cooking oil

3½ qt (14 cups [3 L]) water, for broth

1 large yellow onion, peeled and cut in half

2 lemongrass stalks, cut into 2" (5-cm) pieces and bruised

1 lb (455 g) daikon or carrots, peeled and cut into bite-sized pieces

3 tbsp (45 ml) fish sauce, plus more to taste

2 tsp (4 g) chicken bouillon powder

1 tsp turmeric powder

1 (1" ([2.5-cm], 30-g) piece yellow rock sugar, or 1½ tsp (6 g) granulated sugar

4 tomatoes, quartered

Pork and Shrimp Topping

1 lb (455 g) thinly sliced pork shoulder

¼ cup (17 g) finely minced lemongrass (optional)

4 shallots, chopped

1 tbsp (15 ml) fish sauce

2 tsp (4 g) chicken bouillon powder

2 tbsp (30 ml) Annatto Oil (page 181) or neutral oil

6 cloves garlic, minced

1 lb (455 g) shrimp, peeled and deveined

½ cup (80 g) chopped fresh or canned pineapple (optional)

Salt and freshly ground black pepper

Parboil the Pork Ribs: Slice the ribs into individual pieces with equal amounts of meat on each side. Place them in a large stockpot with enough water to cover without boiling over. Add ½ tablespoon (9 g) of salt and bring the water to a boil, covered, over high heat. This may take up to 20 minutes. Once boiling, cook the ribs for 3 minutes. Discard the liquid and rinse the ribs under cold water to remove the impurities. Transfer them to a large bowl, then season the ribs with 1 tablespoon (18 g) of salt.

Make the Broth: Clean the stockpot, add and heat the oil over high heat, then sear the ribs for 2 minutes on each side. Add the fresh water, onion, lemongrass stalks and daikon. Season with the fish sauce, chicken bouillon powder, turmeric powder and rock sugar. Bring the liquid to a boil over high heat. Lower the heat to low, cover and simmer until the meat is tender, 2 to 2½ hours. Add the quartered tomatoes to the broth. Adjust to taste with more fish sauce, rock sugar or water.

Make the Pork and Shrimp Topping: In a large bowl, season the pork shoulder with the minced lemongrass, shallots, fish sauce and chicken bouillon powder. In a large skillet, heat the annatto oil and sauté the garlic until softened. Add the pork and cook for 3 minutes, or until no longer pink. Add the shrimp and cook for about 2 minutes, or until no longer translucent. Mix in the pineapple (if using) and heat through. Add salt and pepper to taste, and turn off the heat.

(continued)

Quảng-Style Turmeric Noodle Soup (Mì Quảng) *continued*

Noodles

2 lb (905 g) dried flat rice noodles (medium-sized or large)

1 tbsp (7 g) turmeric powder

1 tbsp (15 ml) neutral cooking oil

For Serving

½ head cabbage, sliced (about 1 lb [455 g] sliced)

Fresh Vietnamese coriander, perilla leaves

½ cup (75 g) crushed roasted peanuts

12 oz (340 g) mung bean sprouts

3 large sesame rice crackers, broken into large bite-sized pieces

2 limes, cut into wedges

Cook the Noodles: In a large bowl, cover the dried noodles with warm water for 20 minutes. Boil a pot of water, then add the noodles and turmeric powder. Stir and cook for 1 to 3 minutes, or just until the noodles are al dente. Drain and rinse under cold water. Add the oil to coat the noodles, to prevent them from sticking.

Serve: To each large serving bowl, add a layer of cabbage, noodles, ribs, pork and shrimp. Ladle in 1 to 2 cups (240 to 475 ml) of hot broth, depending on preference. Top with Vietnamese coriander, perilla leaves, roasted peanuts, mung bean sprouts, sesame rice crackers and a lime wedge.

Cambodian Phnom Penh Noodle Soup
(Hủ Tiếu Nam Vang)

This popular pork and seafood noodle soup has origins in Cambodia and influence from China. The pork broth flavor is deepened with the umami of dried shrimp or squid. The "surf and turf" toppings may include ground pork, shrimp, squid, ribs, beef, Chinese BBQ pork or chicken. "Nam Vang" refers to Phnom Penh, Cambodia's capital. The Cambodian soup kuy teav made its way to South Vietnam, where other variations were born. Hủ Tiếu Mỹ Tho hails from the city of the Mekong Delta and includes more seafood; Hủ Tiếu Tàu (Chinese) includes egg noodles; and Hủ Tiếu Khô (dry) is served with the broth on the side and a dipping sauce. Hủ Tiếu can also be served with rice, tapioca, egg, cellophane or vermicelli noodles.

There are fewer rules with Hủ Tiếu soup except that its signature broth is pork based and often sweeter to suit the taste of the South. The following are Mom's recipes for her version of the "wet" and "dry" styles of this soup, inspired by all the above.

Yield: 6 servings

Broth

3 lb (1.4 kg) pork ribs

1½ tbsp (27 g) salt, divided

2 tbsp (30 ml) neutral cooking oil

3½ qt (14 cups [3 L]) water, for broth

1 large onion, peeled and cut in half

1 lb (455 g) daikon or carrots, peeled and cut into bite-sized pieces

¼ cup (20 g) dried shrimp

1 (1" [2.5-cm], 30-g) piece yellow rock sugar, or 1½ tsp (7 g) granulated sugar

2 tbsp (30 ml) fish sauce, plus more to taste

1 tbsp (6 g) chicken bouillon powder

Pork and Shrimp Topping

2 tbsp (30 ml) neutral cooking oil

1 large onion, chopped

1 lb (455 g) ground pork

1 tbsp (15 ml) fish sauce

2 tsp (10 g) light or dark brown sugar

1 tbsp (15 ml) water

1 lb (455 g) shrimp, peeled and deveined

Salt, for sprinkling

Parboil the Pork Ribs: Slice the ribs into individual pieces with equal amounts of meat on each side. Add them to a large stockpot with enough water to cover without boiling over. Add ½ tablespoon (9 g) of salt and bring the liquid to a boil, uncovered, over high heat. This may take up to 20 minutes. Once boiling, cook the ribs for 3 minutes. Discard the liquid and rinse the ribs under cold water to remove the impurities. Transfer them to a large bowl and season the ribs with 1 tablespoon (18 g) of salt.

Make the Broth: Clean the stockpot, add and heat the oil over high heat and sear the ribs for 2 minutes on each side. Add the fresh water, onion, daikon, dried shrimp, rock sugar, fish sauce and chicken bouillon powder. Bring the liquid to a boil. Lower the heat to low, cover and simmer until the pork is tender, about 2½ hours. Discard the solids (or keep the daikon to serve). Skim off the oil and any scum that rose to the top during the cooking process. Adjust the broth to taste with more fish sauce, sugar or water.

Cook the Pork and Shrimp: In a large skillet, heat the oil over medium-high heat. Sauté the onion until softened, about 3 minutes. Add the ground pork, fish sauce, brown sugar and water. Break the ground pork into small pieces and cook for 6 to 8 minutes, or until cooked through. Remove from the heat and set aside.

Lower the shrimp, inside a strainer, into the finished hot broth, holding onto the handle of the strainer while the shrimp cooks, to keep them inside it. Cook for 2 to 3 minutes. Transfer the shrimp to a bowl once they curl into a C shape. Sprinkle the shrimp with salt.

(continued)

For Serving

1 lb (455 g) fresh egg noodles, cooked

1 lb (455 g) dried rice noodles, cooked

6 green onions, sliced

1 cup (59 g) Fried Shallots (page 180)

8 oz (225 g) mung bean sprouts

Fresh Chinese celery leaves or cilantro

½ cup (75 g) crushed roasted peanuts

2 limes, cut into wedges

1 cup (240 ml) Mom's All-Purpose Sauce (page 183, optional)

Serve: To each large serving bowl, add a layer of egg and rice noodles. Add the shrimp, ground pork and pork ribs. Ladle in 2 cups (475 ml) of the hot broth and top with green onion, fried shallots, mung bean sprouts, Chinese celery leaves, roasted peanuts and a lime wedge.

If serving "dry" style, serve each bowl of noodles with 2 tablespoons (30 ml) of the all-purpose sauce mixed with 2 tablespoons (30 ml) of the broth to loosen up the noodles. Add a small bowl of broth on the side for sipping.

Tapioca Noodle Soup with Crab (Bánh Canh Cua)

Several people told me they were excited for a Bánh Canh recipe in my book, so this one's for you! The bone- or crab-based broth has a thicker consistency than other soups. Traditionally, the fresh, chewy tapioca noodles are boiled in the broth and the starches create a naturally thicker consistency that feels luxurious. However, we're using tapioca starch to thicken the broth and the Annatto Oil (page 181) is what gives it that beautiful red-orange hue. Alternatively, you can also add a scoop of crab paste or Sate Chili Oil (page 181) for added flavor. The crabmeat can be replaced with shredded chicken or toppings from the other soup recipes.

Yield: 6 servings

Broth

3 lb (1.4 kg) pork ribs

1 lb (455 g) pork loin

1½ tbsp (27 g) salt, divided

2 tbsp (30 ml) neutral cooking oil

3⅓ qt (14 cups [3 L]) water, for broth

¼ cup (20 g) dried shrimp

1 large onion, peeled and cut in half

1 lb (455 g) daikon or carrots, peeled and cut into 3" (7.5-cm) pieces

3 tbsp (45 ml) fish sauce, plus more to taste

2 tsp (4 g) chicken bouillon powder

1 (1" [2.5-cm], 30-g) piece yellow rock sugar, or 1½ tsp (7 g) granulated sugar

⅓ cup (43 g) tapioca starch plus 1 cup (240 ml) water, for slurry

2 tbsp (30 ml) Annatto Oil (page 181)

Shrimp

1 tsp salt

8 oz (225 g) shrimp, peeled and deveined

For Serving

1½ lb (680 g) dried or 2 lb (905 g) fresh tapioca noodles, cooked

1 (15-oz [425-g]) can quail eggs, for topping

8 oz (225 g) lump crabmeat, for topping

Fresh cilantro, sliced green onion

1 cup (59 g) Fried Shallots (page 180)

2 limes, cut into wedges

Parboil the Pork Ribs: Slice the ribs into individual pieces with equal amounts of meat on each side. Place the ribs and pork loin in a large stockpot with enough water to cover without boiling over. Add ½ tablespoon (9 g) of salt and bring the water to a boil, uncovered, over high heat. This may take up to 20 minutes. Once boiling, remove the lid and cook for 3 minutes. Discard the liquid and rinse the ribs and pork loin under cold water to remove the impurities. Place the ribs and pork loin in a large bowl and season with 1 tablespoon (18 g) of the salt.

Make the Broth: Clean the stockpot, then add and heat the neutral oil over high heat. Sear the ribs and pork loin in the oil for 2 minutes on each side. Add the fresh water, dried shrimp, onion and daikon. Season with the fish sauce, chicken bouillon powder and rock sugar. Bring the fresh water to a boil, uncovered, over high heat. Lower the heat to low, cover and simmer until the pork loin is cooked, about 1 hour. The juices should run clear when you poke it with a chopstick, and the internal temperature is safe at 145 to 160°F (63 to 71°C). Transfer the pork loin to a cutting board and let rest for 10 minutes before slicing. Discard the onion and daikon. Cover and simmer the ribs for 1½ hours longer, or until the meat is tender. Transfer the ribs to a large bowl. Skim off the oil and adjust the broth to taste with fish sauce, rock sugar or water.

In a small bowl, mix together the tapioca starch, water and annatto oil to make a slurry. Pour it into the broth and let cook for 5 minutes to thicken.

Prepare the Toppings: Slice the pork loin thinly and transfer it to a bowl. Pour a cup (240 ml) of the broth on it to keep it moist. To cook the shrimp, bring a small pot of water and a teaspoon of salt to a boil over medium-high heat. Lower the shrimp, in a strainer, into the boiling water, turn off the heat and let cook until they curl into a C shape. Transfer the shrimp to a bowl. Serve the pork ribs on the bone or pull apart the meat.

Serve: To each large serving bowl, add the noodles, slices of pork loin, pork ribs, shrimp, quail eggs and 2 to 3 ounces (55 to 85 g) of crabmeat. Ladle in 2 cups (475 ml) of hot broth. Top with cilantro, sliced green onion, fried shallots and a wedge of lime.

Sour Seafood Soup (Canh Chua)

This seafood soup originates from the Mekong Delta in the South, where freshwater fish is accessible. The tamarind-based broth offers a sweet-and-sour flavor that mellows with the sweetness of the pineapple and the umami from the fish sauce. Taro stems (Bạc Hà), also known as elephant ear, is a spongy plant that absorbs the tangy broth. Catfish is often the fish of choice, but you can replace it with cod or salmon. This light and refreshing soup consists of tomatoes, bean sprouts and rice paddy herbs (Ngò Ôm/om) that have a unique cumin and citrusy flavor. If you can't find taro stems, use celery stalks.

Yield: 6 servings

2 lb (905 g) catfish, cod or salmon steaks or filets

¼ cup (30 g) all-purpose flour, for cleaning fish

6½ tbsp (98 ml) fish sauce, divided

1½ oz (43 g) tamarind pulp

1 cup (240 ml) warm water (110°F [43°C])

2½ qt (10 cups [2 L]) water

1 tbsp (6 g) chicken bouillon powder

1 tbsp (13 g) sugar

20 oz (567 g) canned pineapple chunks (reserve ¼ cup [60 ml] juice from the can)

8 oz (225 g) taro stems, sliced diagonally

4 Roma tomatoes, quartered

For Serving

Fresh rice paddy herbs, cilantro or Thai basil

8 oz (225 g) mung bean sprouts

Cooked rice

Clean and Marinate the Fish: Coat the fish with all-purpose flour to deodorize it. Be careful of any pin bones that stick out. Rinse under cold water, gently rubbing the flour off with your fingers, then pat the fish dry. In a large bowl, coat the fish with 1½ tablespoons (23 ml) of the fish sauce and set aside.

Make the Broth: In a small bowl, combine the tamarind pulp and 1 cup (240 ml) of warm water. Set aside for 10 minutes to soften. Strain the tamarind juice through a sieve into a cup, and discard the seeds. In a 6-quart (6-L) stockpot, combine the fresh water, chicken bouillon powder, sugar, tamarind juice, remaining 5 tablespoons (75 ml) of fish sauce and the pineapple chunks and pineapple juice. Bring to a boil over medium-high heat. Once boiling, add the fish to the pot, lower the heat to low and simmer, uncovered, for 10 minutes.

Carefully transfer the fish to a large bowl to prevent it from breaking apart in the pot when adding the vegetables. Set aside. Add the taro stems and tomatoes to the soup to warm through, about 2 minutes.

Serve: To each large serving bowl, add a piece of fish and ladle in 1½ cups (375 ml) of soup. Top with the rice paddy herbs and mung bean sprouts, and serve with rice.

Note: If you can't find tamarind pulp, you can substitute it with tamarind soup powder mix. Use the amount specified on the package for about 10 cups (2 L) of water.

The Art of Kho
Braises and Stews

"Kho" is the term for a Vietnamese cooking technique; it means to braise, stew or simmer. In many Kho dishes, the magic starts by patiently caramelizing sugar and water to create a Vietnamese caramel sauce (Nước Màu) that deepens the flavor and color of food. The components are then slowly simmered in the sauces, aromatics and a braising liquid that is often water, broth or coconut water.

Braising involves browning meats or vegetables in fat and slowly cooking it in a small amount of liquid. Slow cooking breaks down the connective tissue into gelatin and relaxes the muscle fibers, resulting in tender, melt-in-your-mouth pieces of meat. If braised for too long or without enough liquid, the fat may render out, resulting in dry meat. As with making a soup, the braising liquid is brought to a boil to lock in an effective temperature, then it is simmered, covered, over low heat. Small bubbles should rise and pop at a gentle, controlled, ongoing pace. Stewing follows a similar process, but involves more liquid to submerge the protein. The recipes in this section are perfect to eat with rice, vermicelli noodles or a baguette to sop up the sauce.

Vietnamese Caramel Sauce (Nước Màu)

Vietnamese caramel sauce is less sweet than Western caramel sauce and cooks until it is a dark red-amber color to draw out a distinctive bittersweet taste, similar to dark molasses. It is the basis for many Vietnamese braised dishes, pairing well with the umami of fish sauce. The longer the sugar cooks, the less sweet and more bitter it turns, but be careful, as there is a fine line before it burns. The following method is the easiest, no-fail way to ensure that it doesn't stick to your cooking utensil. Make a jar to save time from having to make it for every dish. Use 2 to 3 tablespoons (30 to 45 ml) for the recipes that require it.

Yield: ¾ cup (177 ml)

1 cup (200 g) sugar
¾ cup (180 ml) water, divided, plus more if needed

In a sauté or sauce pan, mix the sugar with ½ cup (120 ml) of the water, using a wooden or heatproof spatula. Place over medium heat and cook undisturbed. The mixture should start bubbling and turn a light brown color after 3 to 4 minutes. Give the pan a swirl to redistribute the color. It will start to turn a golden red-amber color after about 3 minutes. Lower the heat to medium-low because it will start to cook faster at this point. Turn off the heat when it turns a dark red-amber color, about 2 more minutes. Add the remaining ¼ cup (60 ml) of water to loosen the caramel. Be careful because the water will cause the hot caramel to sizzle. Loosen up the caramel with a spatula, turn the heat back to medium-low and bring it to a boil, 1 to 2 minutes. Turn off the heat and let it cool for 10 minutes. The sauce should still be fluid, but will get more viscous as it cools, and the end result should resemble the consistency in between syrup and honey. If it is too thick, heat the mixture with ¼ cup (60 ml) more water.

Let it cool, then store the sauce in an airtight glass jar. It will last for 1 year in a dark, cool area of the pantry.

Pro Tip: If the caramel hardens, you may have cooked it for too long and too much water evaporated. Heat it on medium-low to reliquefy the caramel and add ¼ cup (60 ml) or more water. Add just a drop of lemon juice or apple cider vinegar to prevent the sugar from recrystallizing. Bring it to a boil and turn off the heat.

Braised Pork with Eggs (Thịt Kho Trứng)

Vietnamese families routinely eat this dish, which is often made in large batches. Chunks of marinated pork and hard-boiled eggs are braised in a caramel sauce, garlic, shallots, soy sauce and an additional liquid until tender. Traditionally, this dish is made during Tết, the Vietnamese Lunar New Year. It could be made in advance and last the week while the streets close down to celebrate the holiday. In the South, this dish is sweeter with the addition of coconut juice, whereas the Northern version leans toward more savory. Some people like more broth, and others like it reduced. This recipe is how I enjoy it.

Yield: 6 servings

Pork and Eggs

8 large eggs

3 lb (1.4 kg) pork belly or shoulder, cut into 1" (2.5-cm) cubes

6 cloves garlic, minced

2 medium-sized shallots, chopped finely

¼ cup (60 ml) fish sauce

2 tsp (10 ml) soy sauce

½ tsp salt

16 oz (475 ml) coconut water, juice or soda

⅛ tsp freshly ground black pepper

Caramel Sauce (Nước Màu)

¼ cup (50 g) sugar

¼ cup (60 ml) water

1 tbsp (15 ml) neutral cooking oil

For Serving

Cooked rice

Steamed bok choy or Chinese broccoli

Boil the Eggs: Place the eggs in a small pot and add enough water to cover by 1 inch (2.5 cm). Bring the liquid to a boil over medium-high heat and cook for 12 minutes. Drain the water from the pot and transfer the eggs to an ice bath or run under cold water. Once cool to the touch, peel the eggs immediately. They will be harder to peel later.

Parboil the Pork: Bring a large pot of water to a boil, then, using a colander or heatproof tongs, lower the cubed pork into the water and cook for 5 minutes. Drain the liquid and rinse the pork under cold water. Set aside in a large bowl.

Marinate the Pork: Add the garlic, shallots, fish sauce, soy sauce and salt to the pork and let marinate for 10 minutes.

Make the Caramel Sauce: In a large pot, mix together the sugar and water. Let cook undisturbed over medium heat. The mixture will start to bubble and will slowly become a dark red-amber color, 5 to 7 minutes. As it cooks, periodically swirl the pot around, if needed, to evenly distribute the sugar water.

Braise the Pork: To the same pot, quickly add the oil to the caramel sauce, then cook the pork over medium-high heat, rotating the pieces to brown in the sauce on all sides, about 3 minutes total. Pour in the residual marinade from the bowl, plus the coconut water and enough water to cover the pork. Cover and bring the liquid to a boil. Lower the heat to medium-low and simmer for 30 minutes. Then, add the eggs and simmer, covered, periodically rotating the eggs for an even color, until the meat is tender, 1 to 1½ hours. Skim off the oil. Adjust the broth to taste and season with the pepper.

Serve: Enjoy over rice served with bok choy or Chinese broccoli.

Pro Tip: If making this recipe with thinner pieces of pork, reduce the simmering time. Pork ribs will take longer, about 2½ hours.

Vietnamese Beef Stew (Bò Kho)

This stew represents home in Saigon. Tender chunks of beef and carrots are simmered in an aromatic broth with lemongrass, shallots, fish sauce, star anise and five-spice powder. Bò Kho is the result of many influences throughout the country's history of colonization, including France with the introduction of beef for consumption, and China with the use of star anise and five-spice. However, it is clear that this family favorite is distinctly Vietnamese, made from once-considered "new" ingredients that became native to Vietnam.

Yield: 6 servings

Beef

3 lb (1.4 kg) chuck roast, cubed into 1½" (4-cm) pieces

1 medium-sized shallot, minced

6 cloves garlic, minced

2 tbsp (30 ml) fish sauce

1½ tbsp (23 g) light or dark brown sugar

2 tsp (4 g) five-spice powder

1 tsp salt

1 tsp freshly ground black pepper

¼ cup (60 ml) neutral cooking oil, divided

Braising Liquid

1 large onion, chopped

¼ cup (65 g) tomato paste

1 tbsp (7 g) paprika

1 (2" [5-cm]) knob fresh ginger, peeled

6½ cups (1.5 L) water

3 lemongrass stalks, center-cut pieces and bruised

3 whole star anise, or ½ tsp five-spice powder

3 bay leaves

1½ tsp (3 g) beef bouillon powder

1 tsp dark soy sauce

2 lb (905 g) carrots, peeled and chopped diagonally into bite-sized pieces

For Serving

Baguettes, cooked rice or 1½ lb (680 g) dried rice noodles, cooked

Fresh cilantro, mint, Thai basil and Vietnamese coriander

Marinate the Beef: In a large bowl, coat the cubed beef with the shallot, garlic, fish sauce, brown sugar, five-spice powder, salt, pepper and 2 tablespoons (30 ml) of the oil. Cover and marinate in the fridge for at least 20 minutes, ideally overnight for best results.

Braise the Beef: In a large pot, heat the remaining 2 tablespoons (30 ml) of oil over high heat. You will be cooking the beef in two batches, to prevent overcrowding the pot. Cook half of the cubed beef in a single layer for a minute on each side, then set aside, with its juices, in a large bowl. Cook the rest of the beef. Sauté the onion in the same pot until softened, about 3 minutes. Mix in the tomato paste, paprika and ginger and cook for a few minutes. Pour in the water and return the beef, with its juices, to the pot. Add the lemongrass, star anise, bay leaves, beef bouillon powder and dark soy sauce. Cover and bring the liquid to a boil over medium-high heat.

Skim off the foam that rises to the top. Lower the heat to medium-low, cover and simmer for 1½ hours. Add the carrots, cover and simmer until the beef and carrots are tender, about 30 minutes longer. Skim off the oil.

Serve: Discard the lemongrass, star anise and bay leaves before serving. This stew can be eaten with toasted baguettes, rice or noodles, plus cilantro, mint, Thai basil and Vietnamese coriander.

Pro Tip: For a different variation, add ½ pound (226 g) of peeled potatoes or sweet potatoes, cubed into 1-inch (2.5-cm) pieces. Add the potatoes about 10 minutes earlier than the carrots and follow the same directions.

Braised Ginger Chicken (Gà Kho Gừng)

This simple recipe results in tender pieces of chicken that are perfectly caramelized. The braising technique allows for the flavors to develop as if you were cooking all day. The fragrant aromatics of minced ginger, garlic, shallots and lemongrass are familiar, yet also complex. This is where the fresh ginger really shines; it has a slightly peppery, spicy and sweet flavor profile that mellows with cooking.

Yield: 4 servings

Ginger Chicken

2 tbsp (30 ml) fish sauce

1 tbsp (15 ml) soy sauce

½ tsp salt

2 tbsp (30 g) light or dark brown sugar

6 cloves garlic, minced

¼ cup (17 g) finely minced lemongrass (optional)

2 medium-sized shallots, minced

1 (2" [5-cm]) knob fresh ginger, peeled and sliced thinly

2 lb (905 g) boneless, skinless chicken thighs

½ cup (120 ml) coconut water

½ cup (120 ml) water

Caramel Sauce

2 tbsp (26 g) sugar

¼ cup (60 ml) water

2 tbsp (30 ml) neutral cooking oil, for panfrying

For Serving

Cooked rice

Steamed vegetables

Julienned ginger

Marinate the Chicken: In a large bowl, combine the fish sauce, soy sauce, salt, brown sugar, garlic, lemongrass, shallots and ginger. Cut the chicken thighs into 2-inch (5-cm) pieces. Place the chicken in the bowl and coat them well with the marinade. Cover and marinate in the fridge for at least 1 hour, ideally overnight for best results.

Remove the chicken from the fridge 30 minutes before cooking, to bring it to room temperature for even cooking.

Make the Caramel Sauce: In a large pot, mix the sugar and water with a spatula or wooden chopsticks. Let cook undisturbed over medium heat. It will start to bubble and will slowly become a dark red-amber color, 5 to 7 minutes. As it cooks, periodically swirl the pot around, if needed, to evenly distribute and cook the sugar water.

Braise the Chicken: In the same pot, quickly mix the oil into the caramel sauce and cook the chicken over medium-high heat for 2 to 3 minutes total, rotating the pieces on all sides. Pour in the residual marinade, coconut water and water, and bring the liquid to a boil. Lower the heat to medium-low, cover and simmer for 20 minutes. Remove the lid, stir the chicken and cook for 5 minutes, or until the liquid reduces slightly and the chicken is cooked through.

Serve: Spoon the chicken and braising liquid over rice and steamed vegetables, topped with julienned ginger.

Caramelized Braised Salmon (Cá Kho)

Cá Kho is fish braised in a sticky, savory sauce. Typically it is made with catfish, but I love using salmon. Traditionally, a clay pot (Tộ) is used to retain heat, but a deep sauté pan or pot will work fine. This recipe is inspired by my mother-in-law who specializes in cooking with seafood. Her family grew up in Nha Trang, a southern coastal city, where fishing was a big part of my father-in-law's life. My mother-in-law has a note-book filled with loose, handwritten recipes from the Philippines, where they sought refuge after the Vietnam War. Making nostalgic dishes provides familiarity, but they also found new tricks in their Vietnamese American kitchen, including the use of all-purpose flour to coat the fish and rinse away its "fishy smell."

Yield: 4 servings

Fish Steaks

2 lb (905 g) salmon or catfish steaks or filets

¼ cup (30 g) all-purpose flour, for cleaning fish

6 cloves garlic, minced

3 shallots, minced

1 (1" (2.5-cm) knob fresh ginger, peeled and julienned thinly

2 tbsp (30 ml) fish sauce

1½ tsp (8 ml) soy sauce

½ cup (120 ml) coconut juice, Coco Rico® soda or coconut water

Caramel Sauce

2 tbsp (26 g) sugar

¼ cup (60 ml) water

1 tbsp (15 ml) neutral cooking oil

For Serving

Cooked rice

Steamed vegetables

1 green onion, sliced

Bird's eye chilies, sliced (optional)

Clean and Marinate the Fish: Coat the fish with the all-purpose flour, which will help remove any fishy smell. Be careful of the pin bones, which are sharp. Carefully rinse the fish under cold water and pat dry. In a large bowl, marinate the fish with the garlic, shallots, ginger, fish sauce and soy sauce for at least 15 minutes.

Make the Caramel Sauce: In a large skillet, mix the sugar and water with a spatula or wooden chopstick. Let cook undisturbed over medium heat. It will start to bubble and will slowly become a dark red-amber color, 5 to 7 minutes. As it cooks, periodically swirl the pan around, if needed, to evenly distribute and cook the sugar water.

Braise the Fish: In the same pan, quickly mix the oil into the caramel sauce, then sear the fish in the sauce, undisturbed, for 2 minutes over medium-high heat. Flip the fish and sear for 2 minutes. Add the residual marinade from the bowl, the coconut juice and just enough water to cover the fish, about 1 cup (240 ml).

Cover the pan and bring the liquid to a boil. Simmer, covered, over low heat for 20 minutes. Remove the lid to let the liquid reduce, and cook until the fish is tender, 15 to 20 minutes longer, periodically basting the fish with the braising liquid. The cooking time depend on the thickness of the fish. Filets take less time.

Serve: Plate the fish with rice and steamed vegetables such as yu choi or bok choy. Spoon the braising liquid over the fish and top with sliced green onion and bird's eye chilies, if using.

Vietnamese Chicken Curry (Cà Ri Gà)

This curry features marinated chicken, carrots and potatoes simmered in lemongrass, coconut milk and Madras curry powder. During the French colonization, access to the international trade routes led to new imports from other countries, including Indian spices, such as curry powder and coconut milk. India's cuisine had already made an impact on Khmer cooking, and in turn, on Vietnam's cuisine after the expansion South. The Vietnamese created their own distinctive version of curry. Unlike Japanese and Indian curry, Cà Ri Gà is thinner, which is perfect for soaking up with toasted French bread. Make this with boneless or bone-in chicken.

Yield: 6 servings

2 lb (908 g) boneless chicken thighs, cut into 1-inch (2.5-cm) pieces, or bone-in drumsticks

6 cloves garlic, minced

1 tsp salt, divided, plus more to taste

2 tbsp (30 ml) fish sauce

1 tsp light or dark brown sugar

2 lemongrass stalks

3 tbsp (45 ml) cooking oil

2 large shallots, chopped

1 medium-sized onion, chopped into 1" (2.5-cm) pieces (optional)

3 tbsp (19 g) Madras curry powder

3 cups (710 ml) water

1 (13.5-oz [400-ml]) can coconut milk

1 tbsp (6 g) chicken bouillon powder

2 small potatoes (8 oz [225 g]), peeled and cut into 1" (2.5-cm) pieces

3 carrots (1 lb [455 g]), peeled, sliced diagonally into 1" (2.5-cm) pieces

For Serving

Toasted baguette, vermicelli or rice noodles

Fresh cilantro, Vietnamese coriander

Marinate the Chicken: In a large bowl, coat the chicken with the garlic, ½ teaspoon of the salt, fish sauce and brown sugar. Cover and marinate in the fridge for at least 1 hour, ideally overnight for best results.

Prepare the Lemongrass: Remove the top 5 inches (12 cm), the bottom 2 inches (5 cm) and the outer two layers of the lemongrass. Cut the stalks into thirds, bruise them and use the outer two layers of the leaves to tie the stalks together.

Braise the Chicken: In a large pot, heat the oil over medium-high heat, then sauté the shallots and onion until softened. Add the chicken and sear for 2 to 3 minutes, rotating the pieces. Add the curry powder to coat the chicken and cook until it becomes pasty, 2 to 3 minutes. Pour in the water and stir until the curry powder dissolves. Add the coconut milk, chicken bouillon powder, potatoes, carrots, remaining ½ teaspoon of salt and the bruised lemongrass. Cover with a lid and bring the liquid to a boil. Lower the heat to medium-low and simmer until the chicken and vegetables are tender, 20 to 25 minutes. Adjust to taste with salt, fish sauce or sugar.

Serve: Enjoy the curry with toasted baguette, vermicelli noodles or rice, plus cilantro and Vietnamese coriander.

Pro Tip: If you'd like to use bone-in drumsticks, marinate the meat with an additional 1½ teaspoons (9 g) of salt. Proceed with the same steps. Add enough water to submerge the meat by 1 inch (2.5 cm). Bring to a boil and simmer until the chicken is cooked through, for an additional 10 to 15 minutes.

Braised Shiitake Mushrooms and Tofu (Đậu Hũ Kho Nấm)

This vegan dish is inspired by both my moms, who often make a version for our ancestors. Every holiday or anniversary of the date my grandparents left this earth, we honor them with a meal and light incense as if we can have a meal together with them in their afterlife. We leave their favorite dishes on the altar. The tofu and shiitake mushrooms are braised in a simple sweet and savory sauce that is perfect as a side or as a meal in itself.

Yield: 4 servings

1 lb (455 g) fresh shiitake mushrooms
4 baby bok choy
3 cloves garlic, chopped finely
¼ cup (60 ml) coconut juice or water
¾ cup (175 ml) water
2 tbsp (30 ml) vegetarian stir-fry sauce or hoisin sauce
1½ tbsp (23 ml) soy sauce
1 lb (455 g) Fried Tofu Puffs (page 39 or store-bought)
Freshly ground black pepper

Caramel Sauce

2 tbsp (26 g) sugar
¼ cup (60 ml) water
1 tbsp (15 ml) neutral cooking oil

Slurry

¼ cup (60 ml) water mixed with 2 tsp (5 g) cornstarch

For Serving

Cooked rice

Prep the Vegetables: Wash the mushrooms and trim the stems level with the mushroom cap, to make it easier to eat. Leave the mushrooms whole, or cut them into halves or quarters depending on their size.

Wash the bok choy and cut them into bite-sized pieces. Keep the hard parts and the leaves separate to cook at different times.

Make the Caramel Sauce: In a large, deep skillet or pot, mix the sugar and water with a spatula or wooden chopstick. Let cook undisturbed over medium heat. It will start to bubble and will slowly become a dark red-amber color, 5 to 7 minutes. As it cooks, periodically swirl the pan around, if needed, to evenly distribute and cook the sugar water.

Braise the Vegetables: To the same pan, quickly add the oil to the caramel sauce and mix in the mushrooms and garlic over medium heat. Pour in the coconut juice and water. Mix in the stir-fry sauce and soy sauce. Let the liquid come to a boil. Gently coat the fried tofu in the sauce. Lower the heat to low, cover and simmer for 15 minutes. In a small bowl, mix the water and cornstarch to make a slurry. Flip the tofu pieces over, and mix in the slurry and hard parts of the bok choy. Cook until the sauce has thickened, about 3 minutes. Toss in the bok choy leaves last, cover and turn off the heat. The leaves should soften without wilting. Add the pepper to taste.

Serve: Enjoy the braised vegetables and tofu as an entrée with rice or as an accompaniment to a main dish.

Queen of Bánh

All Things Batters and Doughs

Mom is the Queen of Bánh, a category of savory and sweet foods made of flours, starches, grains and beans. After 50 years of practice, she has a keen understanding of how flours and starches behave, and her techniques are just as important. Her approach to conquering doughs and batters was the mentality I wanted to embody in life: fearlessly jumping in with conviction and confidence. Failing was half of the victory. The faster she failed, the faster she could succeed.

Mom created the life she envisioned for us. She went from being a high school math teacher in Vietnam to washing dishes at a Chinese restaurant her first week in America. Fortunately, she channeled her panic into determination. She quickly took English as a Second Language classes and brought home books on power electronics for Dad to study for work. Soon after, he secured a job at an electronics repair shop and made himself indispensable. After her second pregnancy, Mom got her degree and became a financial counselor for a local government agency. By the time I was in fourth grade, we moved out of the apartment and into a home with a garden to grow her lemongrass. She accomplished what she set out to do. Her drive and Dad's hustle sparked a fire in all of us.

As mom showed me how to make Bánh Cuốn, I watched her in her element, moving the pan around swiftly, steaming the batter. After she finished making a plate, the batter hit the pan and it sizzled. The heat was too hot; she turned it down. "This is not Bánh Xèo; it shouldn't sizzle." After making several successful rolls, the batter would no longer coat the pan and it kept swishing around as she swirled it. This meant the heat wasn't high enough, so she increased it. *Cooking is interactive.* The following are key takeaways I learned from the Queen.

Look at the dough and feel its texture. You may need to add more water, flour or starches, depending on the quality, age and source of your ingredients. Older ingredients are drier and require more water or oil to achieve the desired consistency. Flours from different brands have various percentages of protein content. The amount of flour doesn't need to be precise. Rather, it depends on the look and feel. If it feels dry and the dough did not form after being mixed, it needs more water. If the dough feels wet or sticky, add just enough flour or starch to handle the dough easily; it should still feel soft and moist.

Filter the water for certain batters. Water changes remove the excess grittiness and slight smell of flour. To do this, the batter is mixed and set aside to rest. The cloudy water that has separated above the batter is measured and discarded. Then, the same amount of new, fresh water is mixed into the batter. Although optional, it makes a big difference for batters with a high ratio of rice flour, such as Bánh Đúc Nóng (page 99), Bánh Bèo (page 104), and optionally, Bánh Cuốn (page 88). The batter was noticeably smoother, less pasty and silkier the more times the water was changed.

Give it time. There were times when I thought I made a mistake, but all I was missing was patience. Resting the batter or dough gives it time to thicken or expand before cooking. Steamed or cooked batter needs a little time to cool off. Otherwise, you may think it is sticky or mushy when it just needs time to let the heat dissipate to feel its final texture.

After making the recipes in this chapter, you will have completed a Bánh boot camp, covering techniques to steam, bake, boil, panfry and deep-fry a variety of batters and doughs!

Bánh Mì Your Way

"Bánh Mi" means "bread," but also refers to the cult-classic sandwich. Its roots stem from the French baguette, but it wasn't until the end of France's rule when the Vietnamese were free to create their version, the one we know and love. The Bánh Mi Chè Cali shop was "our spot" while we waited for my middle sister to finish her violin lessons. She was a lead violinist for Thuy Nga Paris by Night, an internationally recognized music and entertainment production for the diaspora, which was the first time I saw Vietnamese representation in the media. Mom seeded our connection to culture through weekly doses of Little Saigon and buy one get two free Bánh Mi.

Yield: 6 sandwiches

Bread Options
Vietnamese baguette, French bread, Mexican bolillos

Protein Options
Grilled BBQ Pork (Thịt Nướng; page 23)

Lemongrass Chicken (Gà Sả; page 24)

Beef Stir-Fry (Bò Xào; page 27)

BBQ Pork Meatballs (Bún Chả; page 31)

Grilled Pork Sausage (Nem Nướng; page 32)

Pork Meatballs in Tomato Sauce (Xíu Mại; page 145)

Fried Tofu Puffs (Đậu Hũ Chiên; page 39)

Char Siu (Xá Xíu; page 119)

Steamed pork meatloaf (chả lụa; store-bought)

Other Fillings
Pickled Carrots and Daikon (page 182)

Jalapeños, sliced and seeded

Cucumbers, sliced

Cilantro sprigs

Spreads
Vietnamese Mayonnaise (recipe follows) or American mayonnaise

2 (2.7-oz [75-g]) cans pâté

Vietnamese Mayonnaise (Bơ)
5 large egg yolks from store-bought pasteurized whole eggs

1 cup (240 ml) neutral cooking oil

½ tsp salt, plus more to taste

Choose Your Components: Gather the bread and protein of your choice, following the protein recipes as needed. Gather or prep the pickled carrots and daikon, jalapeños, cucumbers and cilantro.

Make the Vietnamese Mayonnaise (If Using): Remove the eggs from the fridge 30 minutes before use to bring them down to room temperature. Use an electric mixer to emulsify the egg yolks until they have become a thickened pale yellow color. That's when it will be a stable-base to incorporate the oil. Pour in just a few drops of oil at a time in a thin stream while mixing on high speed. Let it emulsify and thicken before pouring in another small stream. Repeat the steps until the mayonnaise becomes thick and creamy. If you add the oil in too fast, the mixture won't combine well and will remain a liquid. Stir in the salt and add more to taste. Store in an airtight container in the fridge for up to 5 days.

Assemble the Sandwich: Toast the bread. Slather a layer of mayonnaise and pâté on the top side (or both sides) of the bread. Add the protein to the bottom side, then top with pickled carrots and daikon, sliced jalapeños and bite-sized sprigs of cilantro. Cut the sandwich in half and enjoy.

Pro Tip: The mayo will appear more yellow with a higher concentration of yolks used. The consistency will also be more rich and butter-like which is why this mayonnaise translates to butter (Bơ) in Vietnamese. Add more oil or use less yolks if you like the mayo thinner.

"Steamed" Rice Rolls (Bánh Cuốn)

Bánh Cuốn originates from Northern Vietnam and is enjoyed throughout the country. These delicate, silky, thin rice paper sheets are filled with a sautéed ground pork and mushroom filling. They are brushed with scallion oil, topped with fried shallots and drowned in Nước Chấm. These can also be made without any filling and topped with fried shallots to make Bánh Ướt, an open-faced version of Bánh Cuốn.

Mom's version uses a nonstick pan for a convenience to "steam" the batter with a lid. Her recipe yields the perfect rice rolls that are thin, soft and chewy. "The first one is always ugly," she says. And it's true: The pan is just warming up, the fresh coat of oil is still becoming one with it and the batter is just getting introduced to it. The steamed pork meatloaf can be found at a Vietnamese market in the refrigerated section.

Yield: 12 to 14 rolls

Batter

½ cup (77 g) rice flour

½ cup (64 g) tapioca starch

½ cup (64 g) cornstarch

3 cups (710 ml) warm water (70 to 85°F [21 to 29°C])

¼ tsp salt

1½ tsp (8 ml) neutral cooking oil

¼ cup (60 ml) Scallion Oil (page 180), for brushing

Ground Pork and Wood Ear Mushroom Filling

1 cup (21 g) dried wood ear mushrooms

1 lb (455 g) ground pork

1 tbsp (15 ml) fish sauce

1 tbsp (6 g) chicken or mushroom bouillon powder

1 tsp sugar

1 tsp freshly ground black pepper

2 tbsp (7 g) Fried Shallots (store-bought or page 180)

2 tbsp (30 ml) Shallot Oil (page 180) or neutral cooking oil

6 cloves garlic, minced

1 large yellow onion, chopped

1½ tbsp (23 ml) water

1 cup (130 g) finely chopped jicama

Make the Batter: In a large bowl, combine the rice flour, tapioca starch, cornstarch, warm water, salt and oil. Mix well, then let the batter rest at room temperature for 30 minutes.

Rehydrate the Mushrooms: In a small bowl of water, soak the dried wood ear mushrooms for 20 minutes, or until softened. Drain and chop them into small pieces.

Cook the Filling: In a large bowl, combine the ground pork, fish sauce, chicken bouillon powder, sugar, pepper and fried shallots. In a large skillet, heat the shallot oil over medium heat and sauté the garlic and onion for 2 minutes. Mix in the pork, water, jicama and rehydrated wood ear mushrooms, and cook until the pork is no longer pink, about 5 minutes.

For a vegan filling, try the All-Purpose Vegan Mushroom Filling and Topping (page 111).

Cook the Rice Rolls: It is best to use a light, lidded nonstick skillet for this. Coat the pan with a thin layer of the scallion oil, using a heat-resistant silicone brush or paper towel. Place the skillet over medium heat and, once the oil is hot, stir the batter and ladle ¼ cup (60 ml) of it onto the pan. Swirl the pan until the batter coats it evenly in a thin layer. Fill in the holes with more batter. Cover with the lid for 15 seconds. Brush the scallion oil onto a large plate and quickly flip the pan upside down in one swift motion over the plate to release the cooked rice sheet. Alternatively, run a heatproof spatula around the sheet before flipping over, or lift the sheet up and over to the prepared plate that has been lightly oiled with scallion oil.

Stir the batter before making the next sheet. Periodically brush more scallion oil on the plate and the pan, to prevent sticking. While waiting for the batter to cook, let the cooked sheet rest for 15 to 30 seconds, then add 2 tablespoons (28 g) of the filling in the center and use your fingers to roll up the sheet toward the opposite end to form a filled roll.

(continued)

For Serving

12 oz (340 g) mung bean sprouts

½ cup (30 g) Fried Shallots (page 180 or store-bought)

½ cup (120 ml) Scallion Oil (page 180)

1 lb (455 g) store-bought Vietnamese steamed pork meatloaf (Chả Lụa), sliced

4 large cucumbers, julienned

Fresh lettuce, perilla leaves

Nước Chấm (page 178)

Serve: In a microwave-safe bowl, microwave the mung bean sprouts for 1 minute. Alternatively, blanche the sprouts in a pot of boiling water for 1 minute. Plate the steamed rice rolls and top with fried shallots, scallion oil, sliced pork meatloaf, cucumbers, mung bean sprouts, lettuce, perilla leaves and Nước Chấm.

Mom's Special Steamed Buns (Bánh Bao)

Mom's steamed buns are soft and fluffy, while the filling is packed with a variety of ingredients that make her version extraordinary compared to the typical Bánh Bao in taste and texture. Her secret is in the details. The variety of ingredients provides texture, and sautéing part of the filling adds caramelization. Feel free to make modifications to the filling—as needed, eliminate some ingredients or double up on others—to simplify the process.

Yield: 8 large buns (5-inch [12-cm]) or 16 small buns (2½-inch [6-cm])

Dough

¾ cup (175 ml) milk, at room temperature or lukewarm, plus more if needed

1 tsp instant yeast

½ cup (100 g) sugar

2⅜ cups (300 g) all-purpose flour, plus more for dusting

½ cup (64 g) cornstarch

1½ tsp (7 g) baking powder

½ tsp salt

1 large egg white

1½ tsp (8 ml) fresh lemon juice

1½ tbsp (23 ml) neutral cooking oil

Filling

1 bundle (2 oz [55 g]) dried mung bean thread noodles

4 dried shiitake mushrooms, sliced

2 tbsp (30 ml) neutral cooking oil

2 Chinese sausages, cut diagonally into ¾" (2-cm)-thick slices

2 shallots, minced

3 cloves garlic, minced

½ cup (80 g) chopped onion

⅛ head cabbage, sliced (4 oz [113 g] sliced)

½ cup (65 g) frozen carrots and peas

Make the Dough: In a small bowl, combine the milk, instant yeast and sugar. Let sit for 10 minutes until it bubbles up. In a large bowl, combine the flour, cornstarch, baking powder and salt. Mix in the yeast mixture.

Using an electric mixer on low speed, add the egg white, lemon juice and oil. Once the dough lifts from the sides of the bowl, about 5 minutes, transfer it to a floured work surface. If the dough looks wet, add just enough flour until it is dry enough to handle, but still soft and moist. If the dough seems dry, add more milk, 1 tablespoon (15 ml) at a time. Knead the dough for a minute, then form it into a ball. The dough is ready when you poke it and it springs back up. Then, let it rest in its bowl, covered, until it has doubled in size. This can take from 45 minutes to 1½ hours, depending on the humidity. Set it in a warm place to help expedite the process.

Prepare the Filling: Rehydrate the mung bean noodles and dried shiitake mushrooms by soaking them in a bowl of warm water for 20 minutes. Discard the water. Chop the noodles and shiitake mushrooms into ¾-inch (2-cm) pieces.

Sauté the Filling: In a large skillet, heat the oil over medium heat and sauté the Chinese sausages and shiitake mushrooms for 1 minute. Add the shallots, garlic, onion, cabbage and frozen carrots and peas. Sauté until softened. Set aside to cool.

Form the Dough: Roll the dough into a log, cut into eight equal parts, then form each portion into a ball. Cover and let rest for 15 minutes.

(continued)

Mom's Special Steamed Buns (Bánh Bao) *continued*

12 oz (340 g) ground pork

1 tbsp (15 ml) oyster sauce

1 tbsp (15 ml) soy sauce

1 tbsp (15 ml) sesame oil

1 tbsp (8 g) cornstarch

1 tsp sugar

1 tsp freshly ground black pepper

1 tsp chicken bouillon powder

4 hard-boiled large eggs, cut in half, or 8 quail eggs

Other

2 tbsp (30 ml) white vinegar, for steaming

12 sprigs cilantro, for topping

Combine the Filling: In a large bowl, combine the ground pork with the oyster sauce, soy sauce, sesame oil, cornstarch, sugar, pepper and chicken bouillon powder. Mix into the sautéed filling. Divide it into eight equal parts. Roll each portion into a ball and use your thumb to press the center to make space for a halved egg or one quail egg, then evenly form the meat around it. Set aside.

Assemble the Buns: Cut parchment paper into eight 5-inch (12-cm) squares or have ready eight paper cupcake liners, pressed flat. Set aside.

Using a rolling pin, roll out each ball of dough into a 5-inch (12-cm)-diameter disk with the center slightly thicker. Place a ball of filling in the center of each. Lift up all four sides of the dough and make pleats by bringing up the remaining dough and folding it over all around in one direction. Pinch the dough at the tip. Place each bun on a parchment square or flattened cupcake liner, to prevent it from sticking to the steamer. Place the buns, along with their paper beneath them, 2 inches (5 cm) apart on a steamer tray and spray them with water.

Steam the Buns: Prepare the steamer with water according to the manufacturer's directions. If you don't have a steamer, see page 19 for tips on preparing a make-shift steamer.

Bring the water to a gentle rolling boil over medium-high heat and add the vinegar to the water, which will brighten the color of the buns. Place the tray of buns in the steamer, then cover, partially vented. Steam for 20 minutes, turn off the heat and wait 5 minutes before removing the buns.

Serve: Plate the buns and top with a cilantro sprig for garnish.

Pâté Chaud Meat Pastry (Bánh Pâté Sô)

My favorite pastries from childhood come in a brown paper bag at our local bakery in Little Saigon. On our drive home from the market, I'd snack on them as a kid and get buttery pastry flakes all over my face. I would stare out the window at the name boards, sounding out the words with diacritics in my head. I'm glad Mom taught me how to read Vietnamese even though I gave her a hard time. Let's just say she could sense my frustration because a single word could have several meanings depending on the change in tone. Then there were words like "Pâté Sô," which sounded French, and I was very confused not knowing the history of French colonialism.

This "hot pie" has pâté as the signature ingredient in the filling; it is available in the refrigerated aisle or in a can at the market. If you can't find it, just omit it. We're using a store-bought puff pastry dough to make it quick and easy.

Yield: 24 meat pies

1 lb (455 g) ground pork

1 large onion, chopped

1 tsp garlic powder

1 tsp sugar

1 tsp salt

1 tsp freshly ground black pepper

1 tsp chicken bouillon powder

1 tsp bay leaf powder

2 tsp (scant 1 g) dried parsley

4 oz (115 g) pâté

2 lb (905 g) store-bought puff pastry dough

2 large egg yolks, for egg wash

Cooking spray, for pan (optional)

Prepare the Filling: In a large bowl, combine the ground pork, onion, garlic powder, sugar, salt, pepper, chicken bouillon powder, bay leaf powder, dried parsley and pâté.

Assemble the Pastries: Thaw the frozen puff pastry dough following the instructions on the package. Work quickly with the cold pastry because the butter in it will soften and you won't get the flaky layers while baking if it is too warm. Lay out the puff pastry sheets and cut them into 3½-inch (9-cm) squares.

In a small bowl, stir the egg yolks with a fork.

Take about 2 tablespoons (28 g) of the meat mixture and form it into a rounded shape in the center of a square. Brush the egg wash around the perimeter. Place a second puff pastry square over it. Using a fork, press the dough around the edges to seal the pie, while pressing down with your fingers around the meatball to get rid of excess air. Use a towel to wipe your fingers periodically to keep the outside of the pastry clean of the filling. Repeat with the remaining pastry squares and meat mixture. Brush the egg wash evenly on the tops of the pies. This will help them turn a golden brown while baking.

Bake the Pastries: Preheat the oven to 350°F (180°C). Line a large baking sheet with parchment paper. If using aluminum foil, spray lightly with cooking spray. Then, add the meat pies and bake for 30 to 35 minutes, or until golden brown.

Serve: Enjoy the pastries as a snack or for potlucks. Store any extras in an airtight container up to 5 days in the fridge, or up to 3 weeks in the freezer. To reheat, preheat the oven to 350°F (180°C) and bake for 8 to 10 minutes. To reheat them from frozen, bake for 10 to 12 minutes. Reduce the time by 2 minutes if using a toaster oven.

Savory Rice Flour Pudding (Bánh Đúc Nóng)

Originating in the Northern countryside, this dish was a resourceful meal made primarily from rice flour and water and became a popular dish eaten by choice. There are two versions of Bánh Đúc. The first is a cooled, steamed rice cake cut into squares, and the second is a piping hot "Nóng" sticky pudding that is made conveniently in a pot. Traditionally, it is topped with a sautéed ground pork and wood ear mushroom mixture and coated with Nước Chấm. However, you can also try Mom's Saucy Pork and Shrimp Topping (page 104), as featured in this photo, or my All-Purpose Vegan Mushroom Filling and Topping (page 111) for other variations!

Yield: 6 to 8 servings

Topping Options
Saucy Pork and Shrimp Topping (page 104)

Ground Pork and Wood Ear Mushroom Filling (page 88)

All-Purpose Vegan Mushroom Filling and Topping (page 111)

Batter
1 cup (128 g) tapioca starch

1 cup (158 g) rice flour

3 tbsp (30 g) glutinous rice flour

2 qt (8 cups [2 L]) water, divided, or more as needed, at room temperature

2 tbsp (30 ml) neutral cooking oil

1 tsp salt

2 tsp (9 g) sugar

2 tsp (4 g) chicken bouillon powder

For Serving
Scallion Oil (page 180)

Fried Shallots (page 180)

Nước Chấm (page 178)

Make the Topping: Select a topping option and make it in advance or while waiting for the batter to rest.

Prepare the Batter: In a large bowl, combine the tapioca starch, rice flour and glutinous rice flour. Mix in 7 cups (1.7 L) of the room-temperature water until well incorporated, then let the batter rest for 30 minutes. During the resting period, the batter should settle to the bottom of the bowl. Using a ladle, scoop out the water that has risen above the batter, measure how much liquid has been removed and discard it. Add the same amount of fresh room-temperature water to the bowl and mix thoroughly. Change the water for a total of two times before the end of the resting period.

Cook the Batter: In a large pot, combine the batter with the oil, salt and sugar. Place over medium heat and periodically stir while the batter cooks. Lower the heat when it starts to thicken. Add the chicken bouillon powder and continue to stir, to prevent the batter from burning. When it looks similar to thickened mashed potatoes, add the remaining cup (240 ml) of water or more, and mix until the texture is softer and less dense, like whipped mashed potatoes. The batter will have become slightly opaque, although it will remain off-white. Turn off the heat. The total cook time will be about 12 minutes.

Serve: Spoon the savory pudding into a serving bowl, and ladle the topping mixture on top along with scallion oil and fried shallots. Serve with Nước Chấm.

Vietnamese Sizzling Crêpes (Bánh Xèo)

Mom and her sisters would make these to order for their growing teenaged brothers and couldn't make them fast enough because they ate so many. The name of this savory crêpe comes from the sizzling sound it makes when the batter hits the hot oil in the pan, "Xèooooo." Common fillings include pork, shrimp and bean sprouts, but there are many regional variations. In Central Vietnam, they are known as Bánh Khoái, distinguished by their natural ivory color, crunchier texture and smaller size. Moving south, the crepes are golden yellow, get larger and are slightly sweeter from the coconut milk in the batter and mung bean in the filling. In coastal regions, the fillings contain more seafood.

Both of my moms precook the fillings for extra flavor and add them to the crêpe when it is crisping up. This also streamlines the process if you scale the recipe. The carbonation of club soda helps the batter get crispy!

Yield: 6 large crêpes

Batter

2 cups (316 g) rice flour

½ cup (64 g) cornstarch

2 cups (475 ml) club soda or water

1 cup (240 ml) coconut milk

2 tsp (5 g) turmeric powder

2 tsp (12 g) salt

1 tsp sugar

¾ cup (175 ml) neutral cooking oil, divided

Filling

1 lb (455 g) pork loin or belly, thinly sliced into bite-sized pieces

1 lb (455 g) shrimp, peeled and deveined

2 tsp (10 ml) fish sauce

½ tsp salt

⅛ tsp freshly ground black pepper

3 green onions, sliced

3 tbsp (45 ml) neutral cooking oil, divided, for panfrying

1 large onion, sliced

12 oz (340 g) mung bean sprouts

For Serving

Fresh lettuce, mint, perilla leaves

Nước Chấm with Tomatoes and Pineapple (page 179)

Prepare the Batter: In a large bowl, combine the rice flour, cornstarch, club soda, coconut milk, turmeric powder, salt, sugar and 1 tablespoon (15 ml) of the oil. Let rest for 1 hour.

Cook the Filling: In a separate large bowl, coat the pork slices and shrimp with the fish sauce, salt, pepper and green onions.

In a large skillet, heat 1 tablespoon (15 ml) of oil over medium-high heat and sauté the onion until softened, about 3 minutes. Add the remaining 2 tablespoons (30 ml) of oil, and once hot, cook the filling mixture until cooked through, 3 to 4 minutes. Set aside.

Cook the Crêpes: In a large, lidded nonstick skillet, heat 1 tablespoon (15 ml) of the oil over medium to medium-high heat. Stir the batter and ladle about ⅓ cup (80 ml) into the pan, depending on the size of your skillet and the preferred size of the finished crêpe. The batter should sizzle. If it doesn't, the heat isn't high enough or you need to wait until the oil gets hot. Quickly swirl the pan around so that the crêpe has an evenly distributed layer of thin batter. Fill in the holes with more batter. After 1 minute, add the bean sprouts, cover with the lid and cook for 2 minutes.

Remove the lid and brush 1 tablespoon (15 ml) of the remaining oil on the sides of the pan so that it drips under the edges of the crêpe. Slide the crêpe around to spread the oil beneath it and patiently wait for the crêpe to crisp up, about 3 minutes. If the pan looks dry, add more oil. Place some of the filling on top and cook, uncovered, until it is heated through, 1 to 2 minutes. Fold over the filled crêpe to form a half-moon and transfer to a cooling rack or serving plate. Repeat the steps to cook additional crêpes individually, stirring the batter each time before ladling it into the pan.

Serve: Enjoy immediately with lettuce, mint, perilla leaves and Nước Chấm. Wrap the crêpe with the lettuce and herbs, then dip them in the sauce or eat the crêpe with a fork and knife and mix in the herbs as an accompaniment.

Savory Mini Pancakes (Bánh Khọt)

"Khọt is a Khọt," Mom motioned to her chopsticks, flicking them upward. She was referring to the sound it makes when it hits the cast-iron molds to lift the pancakes out. By the way, this is how I learned Vietnamese growing up—through context and lots of visuals and deductive reasoning. Sort of like the game Pictionary®.

These basket-shaped pancakes have a crispy exterior and a soft, creamy center topped with shrimp and Scallion Oil (page 180). The special cast-iron molds are similar to an ebelskiver or a Japanese takoyaki pan, but we've also made these successfully in a donut hole maker. Mom's secret to a crispy batter is using club soda.

Yield: 20 to 25 mini pancakes

1⅜ cups (217 g) rice flour

¼ cup (32 g) cornstarch

½ tsp turmeric powder

¼ tsp salt

¼ cup (60 ml) coconut milk

2 cups (475 ml) club soda or water, divided

1 tbsp (15 ml) neutral cooking oil, plus more for cooking crêpes

20 medium-sized shrimp, peeled and deveined

Pinch of salt

For Serving

½ cup (120 ml) Scallion Oil (page 180)

Fresh lettuce, mint, Thai basil, perilla leaves

Nước Chấm (page 178)

Prepare the Batter: In a large bowl, combine the rice flour, cornstarch, turmeric powder, salt, coconut milk, club soda and the tablespoon (15 ml) of oil. Let rest for 30 minutes in the fridge.

Cook the Pancakes: Brush all the wells of an ebelskiver pan with oil and heat the pan over medium-high heat. Once the oil starts to bubble, fill the wells half full with batter. Let cook, uncovered, for 3 to 4 minutes. Once the bottom of the batter is almost set, add a shrimp to each mini pancake and lower the heat to medium, if needed. Stir the batter before pouring in more batter to fill each well until it is three-quarters full. Season the shrimp with a light pinch of salt. Cover and cook for 4 to 5 minutes, or until the edges are crispy. Remove the lid and flip over the pancakes to cook for 1 minute. If the pancakes are not crispy, brush more oil in the well and flip it back over to cook for another 1 to 2 minutes. Transfer the cooked pancakes to a plate. Stir the batter before making the next batch.

Serve: Plate the mini pancakes and top with scallion oil. Serve with a side of lettuce, mint, Thai basil, perilla leaves and Nước Chấm.

These mini pancakes are an all hands event. Many people like to wrap the mini pancakes with the lettuce and herbs, then dip them in the sauce. Others like to eat the mini pancakes separately to keep them crispy and eat the herbs and lettuce as an accompaniment.

Pro Tip: Try spooning coconut milk over the mini pancakes for a creamy, sweet and savory combination!

Steamed Rice Cakes—Wet Style (Bánh Bèo)

"Water fern cake," named after its shape, is a specialty of Central Vietnam. The popular "dry" version is a thin rice cake topped with dried shrimp, mung bean and scallion oil. In the Đà Nẵng and Quảng Nam provinces, there is a "wet" variation. The rice cake is thicker to hold the saucy topping. The first time I tried Mom's version of wet Bánh Bèo, I was blown away. The dimples in the center are created during the cooking process when there is enough water in the steamer and enough heat is used. To make the thinner version of Bánh Bèo with dry toppings, simply add less batter to the cups. To steam the cakes, you'll need 30 shallow heat-resistant dipping bowls, silicone baking cups or foil baking cups that are 3 to 4 inches (7.5 to 10 cm) wide.

Yield: 30 rice cakes

Batter

1 cup (158 g) rice flour

3 tbsp (24 g) tapioca starch

2 tbsp (18 g) potato starch or (16 g) tapioca starch

1½ cups (355 ml) room-temperature water

1½ cups (355 ml) warm water (110°F [43°C])

1 tsp salt

2 tsp (4 g) chicken bouillon powder

2 tbsp (30 ml) neutral cooking oil

Saucy Pork and Shrimp Topping

8 oz (225 g) shrimp, peeled and deveined

8 oz (225 g) ground pork

½ tsp salt

½ tsp chicken bouillon powder

1 tsp sugar

2 tbsp (30 ml) neutral cooking oil

6 cloves garlic, minced

1 large onion, chopped

1 cup (240 ml) water

½ cup (65 g) chopped jicama

2 tbsp (30 ml) Annatto Oil (page 181, optional)

⅛ tsp freshly ground black pepper

1 tbsp (8 g) cornstarch plus 1 tbsp (15 ml) water, for slurry

For Serving

Scallion Oil (page 180)

Fried Shallots (page 180)

Nước Chấm (page 178)

Make the Batter: In a large bowl, combine the rice flour, tapioca starch and potato starch. Mix in the room-temperature water and then the warm water. Let the batter rest at room temperature for at least 1 hour or overnight. After 30 minutes, the batter will settle to the bottom of the bowl. Scoop out the water that has risen above the batter, measure how much liquid has been removed and discard it. Add the same amount of fresh room-temperature water back to the batter and mix. Repeat this process once more at the end of the resting period. Mix in the salt, chicken bouillon powder and oil into the final batter.

Make the Filling: Chop the shrimp into small pieces and set aside in a small bowl.

In a large bowl, combine the ground pork, salt, chicken bouillon powder and sugar.

In a large skillet, heat the oil over medium-high heat. Sauté the garlic and onion until softened, about 3 minutes. Add the pork and cook for 4 minutes, breaking it into small pieces. Mix in the water, shrimp, jicama, annatto oil (if using) and pepper. In a small bowl, quickly mix the cornstarch and water to make a slurry. After another 2 minutes, mix the slurry into the pan. Cook until the sauce has thickened and the pork and shrimp are cooked through, about 2 minutes.

Steam the Batter: Prepare a steamer with water according to the manufacturer's directions. If you don't have a steamer, see page 19 for tips on preparing a makeshift steamer.

Bring the water to a gentle rolling boil over medium-high heat. You will be steaming the rice cakes in batches. Brush the interior of your choice of cups with a thin layer of oil and place as many cups as will fit in a single layer on the steamer tray. Cover, and steam the cups for 5 minutes. Stir the batter well before ladling it into the warm cups, filling them three-quarters full. Cover and steam for 8 to 10 minutes.

Remove the lid carefully to catch any condensation, and discard it. Use heat-proof gloves to remove the cups from the steamer and carefully pour out any liquid that dripped into them. The rice cakes will appear sticky at first. Let them cool for 5 minutes, then plate them or serve directly from the cups. Steam the remaining batter as described.

Serve: Top the steamed rice cakes with the pork and shrimp topping, scallion oil and fried shallots. Serve with a side of Nước Chấm.

Shrimp and Pork Tapioca Dumplings (Bánh Bột Lọc Trần)

My niece Emily has requested this snack from her grandma since she was 4 years old. These clear, chewy, translucent dumplings have a simple savory filling and are covered in Nước Chấm. The annatto oil gives it a vibrant red-orange hue inside. Hailing from the former imperial city of Huế, these elegant parcels, meticulously wrapped in banana leaves and steamed, were presented to the emperors. However, because the leaves require much effort to wash and dry, we're sharing the boiling method so you can make them on a whim.

Yield: 20 to 24 dumplings

Pork and Shrimp Filling

8 oz (225 g) pork shoulder or belly (no skin), chopped

1 tsp fish sauce

1 tsp chicken bouillon powder

½ tsp salt

2 tsp (9 g) sugar

2 tbsp (30 ml) neutral cooking oil

1 tbsp (10 g) minced garlic

2 tbsp (20 g) minced shallot

12 oz (340 g) shrimp, chopped

2 tbsp (30 ml) Annatto Oil (page 181)

½ tsp freshly ground black pepper

Dough

2 cups (256 g) tapioca starch

½ tsp salt

1 tsp sugar

1¼ cups (295 ml) boiling water, divided

2 tbsp (30 ml) neutral cooking oil, plus more for oiling hands

For Serving

¼ cup (60 ml) Scallion Oil (page 180)

Fried Shallots (page 180)

1 cup (240 ml) Nước Chấm (page 178)

Make the Filling: In a large bowl, coat the pork with the fish sauce, chicken bouillon powder, salt and sugar. In a large skillet, heat the oil over medium-high heat. Sauté the garlic and shallot until softened, about 3 minutes. Add the pork and cook for 3 minutes. Mix in the shrimp, annatto oil and pepper. Remove from the heat after 3 minutes, or until cooked through.

For a vegan filling, try the All-Purpose Vegan Mushroom Filling and Topping (page 111).

Prepare the Dough: In a large, heatproof bowl, combine the tapioca starch, salt and sugar. Gradually add 1 cup (240 ml) of the boiling water while mixing with a spatula in one direction. The mixture will look like shaggy pieces of dough. Once it is cool to the touch, add the oil to the dough and knead the dough until it becomes smooth and elastic. If it feels dry, add just enough of the remaining hot water, 1 tablespoon (15 ml) at a time, until the texture feels moist. Rub oil on your hands to keep the dough from sticking to it. If it still feels too sticky, add more tapioca starch, 1 tablespoon (8 g) at a time, until the dough is easy to handle. If you see bumps in the dough, rub them out with your index finger and thumb so the dough cooks evenly. Otherwise, you'll notice white spots after it cooks.

Knead the dough into a ball and cover with plastic wrap.

Assemble the Dumplings: Pinch off a 1-inch (2.5-cm) piece of dough. Flatten it into an even 3-inch (7.5-cm)–diameter disk with your palms and fingers. Spoon 1 to 2 teaspoons (2 to 4 g) of filling into the center and fold over the filled dough to form a half-moon. Press the edges to seal tightly. While working, keep the dough covered so it doesn't dry out; otherwise, it can tear easily.

Boil the Dumplings: Bring a large pot of water to a boil. You will be cooking the dumplings in two batches, to prevent overcrowding the pot. Lower half of the dumplings into the boiling water. Use a spatula to gently stir and keep the dumplings from touching each other. When ready, they will appear translucent and float to the top, about 5 minutes. Transfer them to an ice bath for 30 seconds so they don't stick. Cook the second batch and transfer them to the ice bath.

Serve: Plate the dumplings and brush them with scallion oil, top with fried shallots and serve with a side of Nước Chấm.

Deep-Fried Pillow Cakes (Bánh Gối)

"Bánh Gối" means "pillow cake" in Vietnamese because these deep-fried hand pies, or dumplings, look like pillows. Their golden color comes from the use of turmeric powder. Bánh Gối originated in the North, but in different regions they may be called Bánh Xếp because of the way they are folded, or Bánh Quai Vạc, as they look like the handle of a cauldron. When I visit home, Mom sends me off with a huge batch that has been fried and frozen. I love to reheat them in the oven for breakfast. If you don't have time to make the pastry from scratch, use ready-made piecrust dough and continue with the recipe.

Yield: 16 dumplings

Dough

1½ cups plus 2 tbsp (203 g) all-purpose flour, plus more for dusting

¼ cup (39 g) rice flour

½ tsp sugar

½ tsp salt

½ tsp turmeric powder

1 large egg

1½ tbsp (23 ml) neutral cooking oil

½ cup (120 ml) cold water

3 tbsp (24 g) cornstarch

1 tbsp (14 g) unsalted butter, at room temperature

2 cups (475 ml) neutral oil, for deep-frying

Filling

¼ cup (5 g) dried wood ear mushrooms

2 oz (55 g) dried mung bean thread noodles

12 oz (340 g) ground pork

2 shallots, minced finely

½ large yellow onion, chopped finely

¼ cup (30 g) shredded carrot (optional)

2 tsp (10 ml) fish sauce

2 tsp (4 g) chicken bouillon powder

1 tsp salt

½ tsp sugar

2 large hard-boiled eggs, cut into 8 pieces each, or 16 quail eggs

For Serving

Fresh lettuce, perilla leaves, fresh mint leaves

Nước Chấm (page 178)

Prepare the Dough: In a large bowl, combine the all-purpose flour, rice flour, sugar, salt and turmeric powder. Mix in the egg and oil thoroughly. Gradually mix in the cold water and knead into a ball of dough. It should be easy to handle and no longer sticky. If the dough appears dry, add more water. If it is too wet, add more flour. Let it rest for 30 minutes, covered. In a small bowl, mix together the cornstarch and butter, and set aside.

Make the Filling: In a bowl of water, soak the dried wood ear mushrooms and mung bean noodles for 20 minutes. Rinse the mushrooms and noodles under cold water and chop them into small pieces. In a large bowl, combine the ground pork, shallots, onion, shredded carrot (if using), fish sauce, chicken bouillon powder, salt and sugar. Set aside.

Assemble the Dumplings: Dust a work surface with flour and roll the dough into an even ¼-inch (6-mm)–thick rectangle. Brush half of the butter mixture onto the dough. Fold the dough into thirds by bringing the top and bottom to the middle, and roll out the dough once more into a ¼-inch (6-mm)–thick rectangle. Brush the rest of the butter mixture onto the dough. Starting on a long end, roll the dough up tightly, jelly roll style, into a long rope.

Cut into 16 equal parts and roll out each portion into a 5-inch (12-cm)–diameter disk. Add 2 tablespoons (28 g) of filling to the center of each disk and top with a piece of egg. Fold the filled dough over to form a half-moon and pinch the edges together. Press the dough around the filling to remove any air. Make pleats along the curved edge of the dough.

Fry the Dumplings: In a high-sided skillet or deep pot, heat the oil over medium-high heat. Working in batches, deep-fry the pastries at 375°F (190°C) until golden brown, 7 to 9 minutes. Transfer them to a wire cooling rack and let rest.

Serve: Enjoy these crispy dumplings wrapped in lettuce with perilla leaves, mint and Nước Chấm.

All-Purpose Vegan Mushroom Filling and Topping (Nấm Xào)

Use this filling and topping to replace meat mixtures in this chapter. It works great for Pâté Chaud Meat Pastry (page 96), "Steamed" Rice Rolls (page 88), Savory Rice Flour Pudding (page 99), Savory Mini Pancakes (page 103), Steamed Rice Cakes—Wet Style (page 104), Shrimp and Pork Tapioca Dumplings (page 107) and Deep-Fried Pillow Cakes (page 108).

Yield: 4 cups (946 ml)

¼ cup (5 g) dried wood ear mushrooms

3 tbsp (45 ml) neutral oil or Shallot Oil (page 180)

6 cloves garlic, minced

1 large onion, chopped

10 oz (280 g) king oyster mushrooms, diced

4 shiitake mushrooms, diced

¼ cup (33 g) diced jicama, or 1 (8-oz [225-g]) can water chestnuts, diced (optional)

¼ cup (60 ml) water

1 tbsp (15 ml) soy sauce

1 tbsp (6 g) mushroom or vegetable bouillon powder

1½ tsp (6 g) sugar

¼ cup (15 g) Fried Shallots (page 180, optional)

Salt, to taste

½ tsp cornstarch (optional)

Prepare the Mushrooms: In a bowl of water, soak the dried wood ear mushrooms until softened, about 20 minutes. Drain and cut them into ⅜- to ¾-inch (1- to 2-cm) pieces.

Sauté the Filling: In a large skillet, heat the oil over medium-high heat. Sauté the garlic for 30 seconds, then mix in the onion.

Once the onion is softened and slightly browned, about 3 minutes, mix in the oyster and shiitake mushrooms, jicama, water, soy sauce, mushroom bouillon powder and sugar. Cook for 4 minutes, then mix in the dried wood ear mushrooms and fried shallots (if using), cook for 2 to 3 more minutes and remove from the heat. Sprinkle with salt to taste.

Serve: Use as a filling or topping for Bánh recipes. Let cool and store in an airtight container for up to 4 days in the fridge, or for up to 3 weeks in the freezer. It can also be made in advance!

Pro Tip: If you need a wetter (saucy) filling, add ¼ cup (60 ml) of water. If you need it drier, add ½ teaspoon of cornstarch.

Cooking with Love
Đặc Biệt Specials

This chapter celebrates bringing loved ones together over good food. As a busy working mother, Mom had to be resourceful with her time, ingredients and budget. Because of her, I've learned how to cook with flexibility. In between getting her second degree in a new language, working and being a mom, she still managed to make home-cooked meals for her children, to instill our Vietnamese heritage.

Home cooking was one of the ways she saved financially while feeding us better than any restaurant could. Her mindset was she could do more for less, although she didn't count her labor of love—which you could see, smell and taste in her food. The amount of preparation and quality in each dish was apparent. She cooked not because she loved to, but because she loved the people she cooked for.

In Vietnam, there were long periods in history when food and resources were scarce, and even recurring periods of famine. Over two million Vietnamese people died of hunger during the Great Famine of 1945 under the misadministration of French and Japanese occupation. The Vietnam War also took the economy into a crisis. There were times when my parents' families were doing well, and other times when everything was taken from them. My parents took this as a stark reminder to be financially conscious. Nevertheless, when it came to food, we had an abundance on the table. Nothing went to waste and leftovers were transformed into exciting creations. Mom cooked with what was in the fridge and what groceries were on sale. She made food stretch without our knowing. She sliced the meat thinner, cubed the beef smaller and added plentiful vegetables in stir-fries to give us sustenance. Because of her tenacity at work and in the kitchen, we had everything from five-star Michelin meals at home, to braces and music lessons.

Sometimes she used spaghetti for Chinese egg noodles or ketchup for tomato fried rice, and leftovers went into fried or sticky rice. In many ways, her style of cooking, and perspective on life, reflected a core theme of Vietnamese cuisine: turning the ordinary into something extraordinary. As you cook the recipes in this book, give yourself permission to adjust as needed. Understand the spirit of what makes a dish authentic, but don't fret over certain ingredients. The most important part of cooking is nourishing yourself and your family. "Đặc Biệt" means "special." This chapter includes recipes that are perfect for hosting through specific techniques such as flash-frying noodles, making stir-fries and getting that perfect sear on shaking beef. You don't have to cook with expensive ingredients to eat fancy.

Crispy Roasted Pork Belly (Thịt Heo Quay)

My mom, brother-in-law and sister have their own versions of crispy roasted pork belly. This dish is often the main event at a potluck. When they showcase their pork belly right out of the oven, it's as if they know their dish is the showstopper. Here is the original way I learned from Alex, my brother-in-law, which always works! The key for a crispy crust is to dry out the skin, which we achieve by drawing out the moisture with salt, then leaving the pork, uncovered, in the fridge for two days.

Yield: 6 servings

1½ tsp (9 g) salt, divided

1 tsp five-spice powder

⅛ tsp freshly ground black pepper

3 lb (1.4 kg) boneless pork belly slab

1 tbsp (15 ml) white distilled vinegar

For Serving

12 oz (340 g) fine rice vermicelli noodles (Bánh Hoi), cooked

Mom's All-Purpose Sauce (page 183) or Nước Chấm (page 178)

Prepare the Pork Belly: In a small bowl, mix together 1 teaspoon of the salt, the five-spice powder and pepper.

On a cutting board, place the pork belly, skin side down, and make slices 1 inch (2.5 cm) apart across the width of the meat. Rub the spice mixture onto the meat on all sides, except the pork skin side, and into the crevices. Wipe your fingers and be careful not to get any spices on the pork skin.

Flip the pork over and pat the skin dry with a paper towel. Optionally, take a toothpick and poke the skin's surface, making as many holes as you can from end to end. This will allow the skin to puff up when cooking. Try to avoid piercing into the fat beneath the skin and definitely don't pierce into the meat, or else the oils and juices will prevent the skin from crisping up. Pat the skin completely dry and lightly brush with the vinegar. Sprinkle the remaining ½ teaspoon of salt evenly on the skin. Wait 20 minutes for the salt to draw out the moisture, then pat dry. Brush on another layer of the vinegar.

Place the pork on a large dish or tray and keep it, uncovered, in the fridge for 2 days to dry out the skin.

Bake the Pork Belly: Remove the pork from the fridge 1 hour before baking, to bring it down to room temperature. Pat the skin dry. Preheat the oven to 350°F (180°C). Line a large baking sheet with aluminum foil. Place a baking rack on the prepared pan and add the pork to the rack, skin side up. Pat the pork skin dry once more. Pour 1 cup (240 ml) of water in the pan to create steam while baking. This will keep the pork moist. Bake on the middle rack for 75 to 90 minutes or until the internal temperature of the pork is 145°F (62°C). At this time, the skin will not be crispy at all. If there is oil on the skin, pat it dry.

Move the pork about 10 inches (25 cm) away from the broiler heating element so that it doesn't burn. Broil on high for about 15 minutes and patiently keep a close eye on it. The high heat will cause the skin to bubble up, but it can quickly burn if you aren't paying attention.

Serve: Remove the pork belly from the oven and let rest, skin side up, for 10 minutes before slicing through. Serve with fine rice vermicelli noodles and Mom's all-purpose sauce or Nước Chấm.

Hoisin Chicken and Red Rice (Gà Rô Ti Cơm Đỏ)

"Gà Rô Ti" translates to "roasted chicken," even though it isn't traditionally roasted in Vietnam. Instead, the chicken is often panfried and, in the South, it is simmered in coconut milk. Typically, Cornish hens are used, but my version uses chicken thighs for simplicity instead. The sweet and savory marinade has a touch of five-spice and resembles the taste of Chinese roasted duck. It is baked and then broiled to achieve the bubbly browned chicken skin. Our family likes to enjoy it over red rice, which is conveniently just ketchup and rice the way Mom made it.

Yield: 6 servings

Chicken

½ cup (120 ml) hoisin sauce

¼ cup (60 ml) low-sodium soy sauce

1 tbsp (13 g) sugar

1 tbsp (15 ml) honey, or 1 tbsp (15 g) light or dark brown sugar

1 tsp five-spice powder

5 lb (2.3 kg) chicken thighs, bone-in and skin on (9 to 12 pieces)

Neutral oil, for pan

Red Rice

2 tbsp (30 ml) neutral oil

6 cloves garlic, minced

2 large yellow onions, chopped

8 cups (1.4 kg) day-old cooked white rice

1 cup (240 ml) ketchup

2 tsp (4 g) chicken or mushroom bouillon powder

Salt and freshly ground black pepper

For Serving

Pickled Cabbage and Carrots (page 182, optional)

3 Roma tomatoes, sliced (optional)

3 English cucumbers, sliced (optional)

Nước Chấm (page 178)

Marinate the Chicken: In a large bowl, combine the hoisin sauce, soy sauce, sugar, honey and five-spice powder. Clean the chicken, trim the skin and pat dry. Place the chicken in the bowl and coat it well. Don't forget to coat under the skin. Cover and marinate in the fridge for at least 4 hours, ideally overnight for best results. Remove from the fridge 30 minutes before cooking, to bring it down to room temperature.

Bake the Chicken: Line a large baking sheet with aluminum foil. Brush oil on the foil and add the chicken thighs, skin side up. The dense spots will cook faster or burn, so make sure there is just a thin, even layer of marinade on the skin. Bake at 400°F (200°C) for 25 minutes on the middle rack. By this time, the skin will look lackluster. To get a grilled, charbroiled effect, transfer the baking sheet one rack higher and broil for 3 to 5 minutes. Watch it carefully and remove the chicken before the marinade on the skin burns. For boneless chicken thighs, cook 5 minutes less before broiling. When thoroughly cooked, the chicken thighs should reach 165°F (73°C).

Make the Red Rice: In a large pot, heat the oil over medium-high heat and sauté the garlic and onions until softened, a few minutes. Rub the day-old rice in between your fingers and add it to the pot. Mix in the ketchup, chicken bouillon powder, salt and pepper. Turn off the heat.

Serve: Plate the chicken thighs with the red rice. Serve with pickled cabbage and carrots or sliced tomatoes and cucumbers with a side of Nước Chấm.

Char Siu Roasted BBQ Pork (Xá Xíu)

Vietnam spent 1,000 years under Chinese rule, which is why you'll notice many incorporated dishes, such as this red roasted pork. This Cantonese classic, char siu, means "fork roasted" because it is skewered and barbecued. Its sweet, savory and smoky char reminds me of my Chinese roots. It wasn't until I was a teenager that I learned in passing that I'm half Chinese. My grandparents changed their name, Chen, to the Vietnamese translation, Trần, after they left China to escape political turmoil. This was the case for a large population of Vietnamese Chinese. Mom said, "Oops." She reasoned that life got busy and they forgot to tell me! I was shocked but embraced another part of my identity. This natural blending of cuisines is seen with the use of char siu in wonton noodle soup (see Pro Tip, page 150), Bánh Mi and fried rice.

Yield: 6 servings

Char Siu BBQ Pork

¼ cup (60 ml) hoisin sauce

¼ cup (60 ml) honey

2 tbsp (30 g) light or dark brown sugar

1 tbsp (15 ml) soy sauce

1 tsp five-spice powder

2 tsp (12 g) salt

1 tbsp (15 ml) sesame oil

6 cloves garlic, minced

1 tsp Shaoxing wine

¼ cup (21 g) red bean curd with its juice, or ⅛ tsp red food coloring (optional, see Note)

1 (2- to 3-lb [905-g to 1.4-kg]) pork shoulder roast

Cooking oil spray, if air frying

Honey Glaze

2 tbsp (30 ml) honey

1 tbsp (15 ml) water

For Serving

Cooked rice

Steamed vegetables

Note: If you want its signature red color, use red fermented bean curd for a natural option or red food coloring for a more vibrant red. Both are optional and do not affect the taste much.

Marinate the Pork: In a large bowl, combine the hoisin sauce, honey, brown sugar, soy sauce, five-spice powder, salt, sesame oil, garlic, Shaoxing wine and red bean curd (if using). Reserve ¼ cup (60 ml) of the marinade in a separate small bowl, if using the oven method.

Cut the pork shoulder roast into long strips 2 to 3 inches (5 to 7.5 cm) thick. If using an air fryer, cut the long strips in half to fit and cook faster.

Use a fork to poke holes ½ inch (1.3 cm) deep in the pork, then coat with the marinade. Cover and marinate in the fridge overnight, along with the separately reserved marinade (if using). Remove from the fridge 45 minutes before cooking, to bring it down to room temperature.

Make the Honey Glaze: In a small bowl, combine the honey and water, then set aside.

Oven Method: Preheat the oven to 400°F (200°C). Line a baking pan with aluminum foil and pour in 1½ cups (355 ml) of water to prevent the drippings from burning. Place a rack on the pan and lay the pieces of pork, spaced 2 inches (5 cm) apart, on the rack. Discard the marinade the pork chilled in. Instead, brush the pork with the reserved marinade and bake for 20 minutes. Brush it again with the reserved marinade after 10 minutes, and once more after 10 minutes. Then, brush on the honey glaze and broil for 10 minutes. The cooking time is a total of 50 minutes. Check the temperature. I like to remove the pork when it's at an internal temperature of 150 to 155°F (66 to 68°C).

Air Fry Method: Preheat an air fryer to 375°F (190°C) for 10 minutes. Spray the tray with cooking oil. Remove the strips of pork from the marinade, place on the tray and air fry for a total of 15 to 18 minutes. While cooking, flip the pork every 5 minutes and brush on the honey glaze. Check the internal temperature and remove the pork when it reaches 150 to 155°F (66 to 68°C), or air fry for a few minutes longer.

Serve: Let the pork rest for 10 minutes before slicing. Serve with rice and steamed vegetables.

Shaking Beef (Thịt Bò Lúc Lắc) and Vietnamese Garlic Noodles (Mì Xào Tỏi)

These are a couple of my go-to recipes for the holidays. Bò Lúc Lắc got its name because the marinated cubes of beef are shaken in a hot wok to sear all the sides. The tender pieces of beef are served with sautéed onions and bell peppers. Traditionally, the beef is cut into smaller cubes, using more affordable cuts of beef, such as top round, flank and sirloin. If you're feeling fancy, use ribeye steaks, which are my favorite, or filet mignon. Shaking beef is often plated on a bed of watercress with rice, cucumbers and tomatoes. It also pairs perfectly with garlic noodles, which are umami rich and can be made in advance; the flavors develop even more the next day.

Yield: 4 servings

Shaking Beef

2 lb (905 g) beef cut into 1" (2.5-cm) cubes

1 head garlic, minced

3 tbsp (45 g) light or dark brown sugar

2 tbsp (30 ml) soy sauce

2 tbsp (30 ml) hoisin sauce

2 tbsp (30 ml) oyster sauce

1 tbsp (15 ml) fish sauce

1½ tsp (8 ml) sesame oil

¼ cup (60 ml) neutral cooking oil, divided

2 red onions, cut into 1" (2.5-cm) pieces

1 red bell pepper, cut into 1" (2.5-cm) pieces

1 green bell pepper, cut into 1" (2.5-cm) pieces

Freshly ground black pepper

Garlic Noodles

1 lb (455 g) dried spaghetti pasta or egg noodles (Mi)

¼ cup (60 g) light brown sugar

¼ cup (60 ml) oyster sauce

4 tsp (20 ml) soy sauce

2 tsp (10 ml) sesame oil

¼ cup (½ stick [57 g]) unsalted butter

1 head garlic, minced

1 bunch green onions, chopped

Grated Parmesan cheese, as desired (optional)

Marinate the Beef: In a large bowl, coat the cubed beef with the garlic, brown sugar, soy sauce, hoisin sauce, oyster sauce, fish sauce and sesame oil. Cover and marinate in the fridge for at least 4 hours, ideally overnight for best results. Remove the beef from the fridge 45 minutes to 1 hour before cooking, to bring it down to room temperature. This will ensure the beef cooks evenly.

Panfry the Beef: In a large skillet, heat 2 tablespoons (30 ml) of the oil over high heat. You will be cooking the beef in two batches—do not overcrowd the pan, or the beef will steam and not brown. Once the oil is hot, add half of the cubed beef in a single layer, reserving the rest for later. Let cook undisturbed, about 2 minutes. Flip the beef and cook undisturbed for 1 to 2 minutes. Then, quickly shake the pan back and forth for 1 minute to finish cooking the other sides. Transfer the beef to a large serving dish.

Deglaze the pan with 1 tablespoon (15 ml) of water and cook all the red onions and bell peppers over high heat until softened and the onions are slightly browned, about 4 minutes. Transfer the vegetables to the same serving dish as the cooked beef.

To the same pan, heat 2 tablespoons (30 ml) of oil over high heat and repeat the steps to cook the second batch of beef. Transfer the beef to the serving dish and use tongs to toss the beef and vegetables together. Finish with pepper to taste.

Cook the Garlic Noodles: Cook the pasta as directed on the package instructions and set aside. In a bowl, combine the brown sugar, oyster sauce, soy sauce and sesame oil. In a large skillet or pot, heat the butter on low heat and cook the garlic until fragrant, a few minutes. Add the cooked noodles and coat them with the sauce. Turn off the heat. Top with green onions and Parmesan cheese (if using).

Serve: Plate the beef and vegetables with a side of garlic noodles.

Hoisin Shrimp (Tôm Tương Đen)

Every birthday, holiday and in between, my family feasts on a platter of Mom's shallow-pan fried shrimp to celebrate. This dish never grows old. The hoisin sauce mixed with the cornstarch creates a savory crust on the shrimp. Our family likes to enjoy the lip-smacking sauce on the shrimp shells and then discard them, but if the shells are thin enough, we like to eat them whole—from the head to the tail. Of course, Mom made this for my traditional Vietnamese engagement party, which she insisted on catering herself because it was how she expressed her love to me, my husband and our loved ones.

Yield: 4 servings

1 lb (455 g) medium-sized shrimp, shells on or off, deveined

1 tsp garlic powder

1 tsp chicken bouillon powder

½ tsp freshly ground black pepper

¼ cup (32 g) cornstarch

¼ cup (60 ml) cooking oil, divided

½ yellow onion, sliced

¼ cup (60 ml) hoisin sauce

3 green onions, chopped into 2" (5-cm) pieces

1 head garlic, minced

2 tbsp (30 ml) water (optional)

For Serving

1 lb (455 g) cooked egg noodles, cooked rice or 4 baby bok choy

Prepare the Shrimp: In a large bowl, season the shrimp with the garlic powder, chicken bouillon powder and pepper. Coat the shrimp with the cornstarch.

Panfry the Shrimp: In a large skillet, heat 1 tablespoon (15 ml) of the oil over medium-high heat and sauté the onion for 3 minutes. Push the onion to the perimeter of the pan. Add the remaining 3 tablespoons (45 ml) of oil in the center and cook the shrimp undisturbed for 1 minute to develop a crust.

Flip the shrimp over and cook undisturbed for 1 minute. Add the hoisin sauce, green onions and garlic. Quickly toss the shrimp to coat, and shake them in the pan to cook for about 1 minute longer. The sauce and cornstarch will make a great crust.

Optionally, add the water to deglaze the pan over medium heat. Mix in the egg noodles, rice or vegetables to pick up the residual sauce.

Serve: Place the platter of shrimp at the table to share. Or plate the shrimp over rice or egg noodles.

House Special Fried Rice (Cơm Chiên Đặc Biệt)

Dad was in charge of making rice and he made it in the rice cooker like clockwork every day. Many cultures have their own version of fried rice. For our household, it was an affordable, fast and comforting way to use up leftovers. Although fried rice is typically a "throw everything you have" in a hot wok or pan, there are simple tricks to make it special. First, rub the day-old rice in between your fingers to separate the clumps after refrigeration. Cook over high heat, and cook quickly to prevent the rice from steaming and getting mushy. Cook the eggs last, so they don't overcook. Take these notes and make your own version of this dish using your favorite ingredients.

Yield: 4 servings

6 cups (1 kg) day-old cooked rice

2 tbsp (30 ml) neutral cooking oil, divided

6 cloves garlic, minced

3 Chinese sausages (Lạp Xưởng), sliced

8 oz (225 g) Char Siu Roasted BBQ Pork (page 119), diced (optional)

8 oz (225 g) shrimp, peeled and deveined

1 large yellow onion, chopped

1½ cups (180 g) frozen carrots and peas (optional)

5 large eggs

1½ tbsp (23 ml) soy sauce

1½ tsp (3 g) chicken bouillon powder

1 tsp sugar

Salt and freshly ground black pepper

For Serving

4 green onions, sliced

2 tbsp (30 ml) Sate Chili Oil (page 181 or store-bought)

Prepare the Rice: In a large bowl, rub the day-old cooked rice through your fingers to separate the rice grains.

Cook the Meat: In a large skillet or wok, heat 1 tablespoon (15 ml) of the oil over medium-high heat. Sauté the garlic, Chinese sausages and BBQ pork for 2 minutes. Make room in the center to add and cook the shrimp for a minute and flip them over. Mix the proteins together and transfer to a large bowl, leaving the oil in the pan.

Make the Fried Rice: In the same pan, sauté the onion in the residual oil over high heat until it softens and starts to develop color on the edges, 4 to 5 minutes. Add the rice and frozen carrots and peas (if using), and cook for 5 minutes. Create a well in the center and add the remaining tablespoon (15 ml) of oil. Add and stir the eggs in the well, then cook undisturbed for 1 minute before folding them over to cook the other side. Gently incorporate the eggs into the rice, breaking the eggs into bite-sized pieces along the way.

Season with soy sauce, chicken bouillon powder and sugar, and adjust to taste. Incorporate the sautéed Chinese sausage, BBQ pork and shrimp last to heat through. Add salt and pepper to taste.

Serve: Plate the fried rice and top with green onions and sate chili oil.

Crispy Fried Noodles (Mì Xào Giòn/Dòn)

This was the first dish Mom taught me how to cook when I was in middle school. She gave me the Chinese egg noodles and instructed me to lower them into the hot oil. They expanded instantly before my eyes. The intertwined egg noodles are flash-fried in the shape of a bird's nest. The stir-fry and gravy coat the extra-crispy noodles that retain their crunch. There are various types of egg noodles in different sizes. Noodles using chicken eggs may have a more vibrant yellow color.

Yield: 6 servings

Shrimp (or Mushrooms)

1 tbsp (15 ml) neutral cooking oil

1 lb (455 g) shrimp, peeled and deveined

¼ tsp salt

6 cloves garlic, minced

Sauce

3 tbsp (24 g) cornstarch

2 tsp (4 g) chicken or mushroom bouillon powder

2 tbsp (30 ml) soy sauce

2 tbsp (30 ml) oyster sauce

1 tsp sugar

2 cup (475 ml) water

Vegetables for Stir-Fry

1 tbsp (15 ml) neutral cooking oil

1 large yellow onion, cut into 1" (2.5-cm) pieces

1 red bell pepper, cut into 1" (2.5-cm) pieces

3 carrots, sliced diagonally

8 baby bok choy, cut into 1" (2.5-cm) pieces

¼ cup (60 ml) water

Salt and freshly ground black pepper

Noodles

1 lb (455 g) fresh wonton or egg noodles

2 to 3 cups (475 to 710 ml) neutral cooking oil, for frying

Cook the Shrimp: In a large, deep skillet or wok, heat the oil over medium-high heat. Place the shrimp in a single layer and season with salt. After 1 minute, add the garlic to the pan and flip the shrimp over. Cook for 1 minute and give them a quick mix. Set the shrimp and garlic aside in a bowl.

Mix the Sauce: In a small bowl, combine the cornstarch, chicken bouillon powder, soy sauce, oyster sauce and sugar. Stir in the water, a little at a time, until the sauce is mixed evenly, then set aside.

Make the Stir-Fry: In the same skillet, heat the oil over medium-high heat. Cook the onion and bell pepper first until softened, about 3 minutes. Next, add the carrots and stems of the bok choy, plus the water. Cover and cook until the carrots are tender, 3 to 4 minutes. Pour in the sauce and let it thicken, about 3 minutes. Mix in the bok choy leaves and shrimp, and heat through for 1 minute. Turn off the heat. Add salt and pepper to taste.

Fry the Noodles: Loosen up the wonton noodles and brush off the excess flour. Divide them into six or more portions, depending on the desired size of the bird's nests. Use a large wok or large, deep pot that is wide enough for the noodles to fry and expand to their fullest. Add at least a 3-inch (7.5-cm) depth of oil and heat over medium-high heat.

Working in batches—don't add too many noodles, or they won't expand and cook evenly—deep-fry the egg noodles at 380°F (193°C) until light golden brown and crispy, about 15 seconds. Flip the noodles and cook for 10 seconds. Be careful not to overcook them, as the noodles will continue to cook after being removed from the oil. Quickly transfer to a cooling rack or a paper towel–lined plate to remove the excess oil.

Serve: Top the deep-fried noodles with the stir-fry and gravy.

Panfried Rice Noodles with Beef Stir-Fry (Phở Áp Chảo)

The "Phở" in this dish refers to the flat rice noodles. The panfried noodle cake is crispy on the outside and chewy on the inside and gets coated in gravy without getting soggy. Fresh rice noodles are convenient and work perfectly for this dish, but I actually prefer the texture of the dried noodles. Because the fresh noodles are presteamed, the inside of the noodle cake is softer. If you nail down the following technique for the dried noodles, you can control the cooking so that the outside of the noodle cake is crispy and the inside stays chewy.

Yield: 4 servings

Beef

1 lb (455 g) beef sirloin, sliced thinly

1 tbsp (15 ml) fish sauce

1 tbsp (15 ml) soy sauce

1 tbsp (15 ml) oyster sauce

1 tbsp (15 ml) hoisin sauce

1 tsp sugar

1 tsp cornstarch

6 cloves garlic, minced

Sauce

1½ tbsp (23 ml) soy sauce

1½ tbsp (23 ml) oyster sauce

1 tsp sugar

2 tsp (4 g) chicken or mushroom bouillon powder

1½ cups (355 ml) water

3 tbsp (24 g) cornstarch

Vegetables for Stir-Fry

1 tbsp (15 ml) neutral cooking oil

1 large yellow onion, sliced

2 large carrots, sliced thinly

8 (8-oz [225-g]) baby bok choy, cut into 1" (2.5-cm) pieces

2 Chinese celery, stems chopped and leaves reserved

4 Roma tomatoes, cut into bite-sized pieces

Salt and freshly ground black pepper

Noodles

1 lb (455 g) dried or 2 lb (905 g) fresh large or extra-large rice noodles or fresh rice sheets

Neutral cooking oil, for frying

Marinate the Beef: In a large bowl, coat the beef with the fish sauce, soy sauce, oyster sauce, hoisin sauce, sugar, cornstarch and garlic. Cover and marinate in the fridge for at least 30 minutes, ideally overnight for best results.

Mix the Sauce: In a small bowl, combine the soy sauce, oyster sauce, sugar, chicken bouillon powder, water and cornstarch. Set aside.

Make the Stir-Fry: In a large skillet, heat the oil over medium-high heat and sauté the onion until softened, about 3 minutes. Add the beef and cook undisturbed for 3 minutes, flipping halfway through that time. Transfer to a plate. Pour the sauce into the pan and cook the carrots, bok choy and Chinese celery stems until softened, 3 to 4 minutes. Add the tomatoes and cook for 1 to 2 minutes. Return the beef and its juices to the stir-fry to warm through, then turn off the heat. Top with the Chinese celery leaves and add salt and pepper to taste.

Prep the Noodles: In a large bowl, soak the dried noodles in hot water for 15 to 20 minutes, or until al dente. When you pull both ends, the noodles should feel softer, but springy without breaking. Drain and let them sit in a colander. Pat dry and add 1 teaspoon of oil to the noodles to prevent sticking.

If using fresh noodles, peel the fresh noodles apart. If using fresh rice sheets, slice them into ½-inch (1.3-cm)–wide noodles.

Panfry the Noodles: You will be making four noodle cakes, one at a time. In a 10- to 12-inch (25- to 30-cm) nonstick skillet, combine 1 tablespoon (15 ml) of water and 1 to 2 tablespoons (15 to 30 ml) of oil to cover the pan evenly. Spread out one-quarter of the dried noodles, intertwining them to form a 1-inch (2.5-cm)-thick noodle cake in an even layer. Cook over medium heat and press them down onto the pan with a spatula. Cover for 2 minutes. The water will create steam to soften the hard parts. Remove the lid and cook until light golden and crispy, 8 to 10 minutes. Flip the noodle cake over, add another tablespoon (15 ml) of oil and swirl the pan to coat it with the oil beneath the noodles. Press the noodles down and cook for 6 to 8 minutes. Adjust the heat and add more oil, if needed, to prevent the noodles from burning. Transfer the fried noodle cake to a cooling rack to keep it crispy until ready to serve. Repeat the steps to cook each remaining noodle cake, one by one.

If using fresh noodles, follow the same process, except omit the water and cook, uncovered, for 10 minutes on one side. Then, flip and cook for 6 to 8 minutes.

Serve: Cut the noodle cakes into large squares or pieces to make them easy to eat. Plate and top with the stir-fry.

Sticky Rice with Chinese Sausage (Xôi Lạp Xưởng)

Throughout my childhood summers, I woke up to a large plate of sticky rice with sliced browned Chinese sausages topped with scallion oil, fried shallots and pork floss. Before Mom left for work, she left a bottle of Maggi® Seasoning sauce on the table for a light drizzle. This plate reminds her of breakfasts growing up in Vietnam. A bonus is that she could whip it up quickly for us, and yet it had the illusion of taking a long time to cook. Throw your leftovers, shredded chicken, eggs, sautéed mushrooms or pork floss into it.

Yield: 2 servings

1 cup (185 g) uncooked glutinous rice

1 tbsp (15 ml) neutral cooking oil, to cook sausages, plus more for brushing steamer

3 Chinese sausages (Lạp Xưởng), sliced diagonally

For Serving

¼ cup (15 g) Fried Shallots (page 180)

¼ cup (60 ml) Scallion Oil (page 180)

Maggi Seasoning or soy sauce

Soak the Sticky Rice: In a large bowl, soak the glutinous rice in enough water to top the rice by 3 inches (7.5 cm) for at least 4 hours, or preferably overnight. Rinse it under cold water to remove excess starches, to prevent clumping when cooked.

Steam the Sticky Rice: Prepare the steamer with water according to the manufacturer's directions. If you don't have a steamer, see page 19 for tips on preparing a makeshift steamer.

Bring the water to a gentle rolling boil over medium-high heat. Brush the steamer tray with oil or line it with parchment paper, to prevent sticking. Place the rice on top of the tray and put it in the steamer. Cover and steam for 20 to 25 minutes.

Sauté the Chinese Sausages: In a skillet, heat the oil over medium heat and sauté the sliced Chinese sausages for a few minutes, until they develop a little brown color and some of their fat renders out.

Serve: Plate the sticky rice and top with fried shallots, Chinese sausage and scallion oil. Top with a drizzle of Maggi Seasoning or soy sauce.

Turmeric and Dill Fish (Chả Cá Thăng Long)

My grandmother's favorite dish from Hanoi is refined, just like her demeanor. Also known as Chả Cá Lã Vọng and Chả Cá Hà Nội, this Northern specialty originiated almost a century ago at the Lã Vọng restaurant, served tableside on a sizzling pan. The chunks of turmeric-marinated white fish are nestled in a bed of sautéed onion, green onions and heaping amounts of sautéed dill. It is a harmony of salty, tangy and sweet with an additional kick of fermented shrimp paste (Mắm Tôm). Feel free to replace with Nước Chấm (page 178).

Yield: 4 servings

Fish

6 cloves garlic, minced

3 tbsp (45 ml) plain yogurt

1½ tsp (8 ml) fish sauce

2 tsp (5 g) turmeric powder

1 tsp chicken bouillon powder

1 tsp sugar

½ tsp salt

2 lb (905 g) cod, tilapia or any white fish filet

¼ to ½ cup (60 to 120 ml) neutral cooking oil, as needed, for panfrying

½ large yellow onion, sliced

6 green onions, cut into 2" (5-cm) pieces

1½ cups (15 g) fresh dill, stems removed and discarded, chopped

Fermented Shrimp Paste Sauce (Mắm Tôm)

3 tbsp (45 g) fermented shrimp paste

2 tbsp (26 g) sugar

2 tbsp (30 ml) water, or more to taste

2 tbsp (30 ml) fresh lime juice (from 1 lime)

3 cloves garlic, minced

1 tbsp (15 ml) chili sauce

For Serving

12 oz (340 g) dried rice vermicelli noodles, cooked, or cooked rice

Crushed roasted peanuts

Sesame rice crackers

Clean and Marinate the Fish: In a large bowl, combine the garlic, yogurt, fish sauce, turmeric powder, chicken bouillon powder, sugar and salt. Clean the fish under cold water, pat dry and cut into 2-inch (5-cm) pieces. Place the fish in the bowl and coat it well. Cover and marinate in the fridge for 15 minutes.

Make the Sauce: In a small bowl, combine the fermented shrimp paste, sugar, water, lime juice, garlic and chili sauce. Adjust to taste by adding more water, lime juice or sugar.

Panfry the Fish: In a large nonstick skillet, heat 3 tablespoons (45 ml) of the oil over medium to medium-high heat. Wipe the excess yogurt off the fish so it doesn't burn. Place the pieces in a single layer on the pan, cooking them in two batches, if needed. To get a nice crust on the fish, let it cook undisturbed for about 4 minutes on each side. The fish should easily lift off the pan when it is ready to flip. Throughout the process, add more oil as needed. Transfer to a plate.

After all the fish is cooked and removed from the pan (see Note), heat 1 tablespoon (15 ml) of oil in the same skillet over medium-high heat. Sauté the onion until it starts to brown, about 3 minutes. Add the green onions and dill and let cook until slightly wilted.

Turn off the heat and plate the onion mixture. Carefully place the fish on top.

Serve: Enjoy with vermicelli noodles or rice, topped with roasted peanuts, sesame rice crackers and a side of fermented shrimp paste sauce or Nước Chấm.

Note: You need to cook the onion, green onions and dill after the fish is removed from the pan because, otherwise, any caramelized bits or residue sticking to the pan will cause the fish to stick to it and either burn or fall apart.

Food on the Streets of Vietnam

Appetizers, Snacks and
Plates to Share

Besides breakfast, lunch and dinner, food is enjoyed all day and night on the streets of Vietnam.

At home, Mom would feed us all day and refer to snacks as "Món Ăn Chơi," which means "eating for fun" (in between regular meals). Dad, on the other hand, would say it's time to Nhậu when he was in a cheerful mood. Vietnam has a strong Nhậu culture, which involves communal imbibing over good food, company and conversation. To "Nhậu" is to drink and eat in a social setting, and it has a celebratory connotation. Hearing my parents use these terms felt light; it meant they could take a breather. I had a strong desire to explore their lives during the Vietnam War, but also independent of it.

Dad describes Saigon as a lively big city with compact, tight-knit streets. He recalls being able to step outside his home and walk just a block away to major streets. Families sold their food specialties in front of their homes or in mobile carts. Restaurants were open as if the owners never slept. What about the Nhậu scene? As young adults, my parents didn't have time to go out often in between finishing their higher education and beginning their careers. Before Dad fought in the war, he moved from Huế to Saigon for college and paved his own path. He specialized in community programs and taught extracurricular activities for youth. Mom received her teaching credential in math and taught high school while working for the South Vietnamese government as a community liaison. When Mom was a child, she often snuck away after school to wander the streets, full of food vendors. She would find herself mesmerized and lose track of time. Her brothers would search for her in the usual spots and bring her home. Her punishment? English and math assignments from Grandpa, who was a school principal. He took whatever opportunity he could to prepare his kids for the future.

What were some of their favorite childhood snacks? They both gave me unexpected answers: tropical fruits, yams, smoothies, candy, street corn, all types of Bánh and Chè (see page 157 for more about Chè). Mom would spend her small change to buy small handheld foods that she didn't get to eat often at home.

Although those snacks were their favorites, mine were associated with my childhood memories of Mom frying up shrimp sweet potato fritters, rolling up fresh spring rolls and grilling smoky ground beef wrapped in betel leaves.

Khai Vị are appetizers that can turn into a full meal when served with noodles or rice. Vice versa, the entrées in this book can be eaten as an appetizer or snack and may also be considered street food eaten around the clock. In this chapter, I've included some of my favorites.

Fresh Spring Rolls with Shrimp and Pork (Gỏi Cuốn)

These light and refreshing rolls are filled with shrimp, slices of juicy pork, vermicelli, lettuce and herbs, dipped in a creamy peanut sauce. Technically, the direct translation is "salad roll," but they go by a number of aliases. I grew up calling them spring rolls, but they are also called fresh spring rolls or summer rolls to differentiate them from fried spring rolls (often known as egg rolls). This confusion may be why some call them rice paper rolls or fresh rolls. Whatever you call them, we can agree that Gỏi Cuốn is an appetizer that you can't pass up.

Yield: 16 rolls

25 large shrimp, peeled and deveined

4 tsp (24 g) salt, divided

1½ lb (680 g) pork shoulder or pork belly (with or without skin)

1½ tsp (6 g) sugar

30 round rice paper sheets, each 8¾" (22 cm) in diameter

2 heads romaine lettuce

1 lb (455 g) dried rice vermicelli noodles, cooked

3 large cucumbers, cut in half and julienned

1 bunch Vietnamese coriander, mint or cilantro

2 bunches chives

For Serving
Peanut Sauce (page 183)

Boil the Shrimp: Bring a small pot of water to a boil. Cook the shrimp in the boiling water with 1 teaspoon of salt for about 1½ minutes, then rinse under cold water. Slice the shrimp in half and set aside.

Boil the Pork: In a large pot, combine the pork shoulder, 1 tablespoon (18 g) of the salt, sugar and enough water to submerge the pork. Bring the liquid to a boil over medium-high heat. Lower the heat, cover and simmer over medium-low heat for 30 to 40 minutes, or until tender. Rinse the pork shoulder under cold water, let rest for 10 minutes, then slice into thin pieces.

Assemble the Rolls: Wet a sheet of rice paper with water and shake off the excess liquid. Lay it on a plate. Cut a lettuce leaf to fit in a line 2 inches (5 cm) from the bottom of the rice paper sheet with 1 inch (2.5 cm) clear on both the left and right sides. Use the lettuce as a vessel for a small portion of the noodles, cucumbers and your choice of Vietnamese coriander, mint or cilantro. On the space above the lettuce, place three shrimp, pink side facing down. Add three slices of pork on top of the shrimp. Roll the rice paper over the vegetables and herbs, fold the right and left sides in, then add a chive with 2 inches (5 cm) sticking out. Continue to roll the rice paper over the shrimp and pork, and keep rolling until it seals.

Serve: Enjoy the fresh spring rolls with peanut sauce.

Fried Spring Rolls (Chả Giò / Nem Rán)

My mother-in-law makes hundreds of fried spring rolls at a time as care packages for her kids. Her secret is using a lot of carrots for sweetness and texture. Originating in China, these were served during the Lunar New Year, the start of spring. Although many, including me, call these egg rolls, technically they are not. The spring roll wrapper is made of wheat flour and results in thin, crispy layers when fried. The "egg roll" is an American Chinese variation that contains egg in the wrapper. It has a thicker, bumpy exterior, while the inner layer is chewy. Make sure you purchase the right wrapper.

Yield: 35 rolls

½ cup (10 g) dried wood ear mushrooms

2 bundles (4 oz [113 g]) dried mung bean thread noodles

4 cups (480 g) shredded carrots (8 medium-sized carrots)

1 tbsp (13 g) + ½ tsp sugar, divided

2 tsp (12 g) salt, divided

1 lb (455 g) ground pork

8 oz (225 g) shrimp, chopped roughly

1 tsp oyster sauce

2 tsp (10 ml) sesame oil

1 tsp garlic powder

1 tsp ground white or freshly ground black pepper

1 large yellow onion, chopped

2 green onions, minced (optional)

1 large egg, for sealing wrappers

1 (40-sheet) package (7.5" [19-cm] square) crispy spring roll wrappers

Neutral cooking oil, for frying

For Serving
Fresh lettuce

Nước Chấm (page 178) or sweet chili sauce

Prepare the Filling: In a bowl of water, submerge the dried wood ear mushrooms and dried mung bean thread noodles until softened, about 20 minutes. Drain and cut them into ⅜- to ¾-inch (1- to 2-cm) pieces.

In a separate bowl, combine the carrots, ½ teaspoon of the sugar and ½ teaspoon of the salt, to draw out the excess moisture. The liquid should release after 10 minutes. Meanwhile, in a large bowl, combine the ground pork, shrimp, remaining 1½ teaspoons (9 g) of salt, remaining tablespoon (13 g) of sugar, oyster sauce, sesame oil, garlic powder, white pepper, onion, green onions and the mung bean noodles and mushrooms. Squeeze out the liquid from the carrots and add them to the filling mixture.

Mix the Egg Wash: Into a small bowl, crack the egg, then stir it with a fork. This will be used to seal the wrappers.

Assemble the Rolls: Place a square wrapper face down, positioned like a diamond. Add ¼ cup (55 g) of filling in a horizontal line 1 inch (2.5 cm) from the lowest corner. Fold that corner tightly over and around the filling. Roll tightly until you reach the widest length of the wrapper. Fold the left and right sides toward the center and continue to roll up until you reach the upper corner of the wrapper. Brush the egg wash on that corner and fold it over the roll to seal. Transfer the rolls, in a single layer, to a tray. Place a sheet of parchment paper or plastic wrap over the rolls if you need to stack more on top. This will prevent the wrappers from sticking to each other.

Fry the Rolls: Fill a large, deep pot with neutral cooking oil to a depth of at least 2 inches (5 cm) and heat over medium-high heat. Fry the rolls in batches at 350°F (180°C), periodically rotating them to cook evenly, until golden brown, 12 to 15 minutes. The internal temperature of the cooked ground pork should reach 160°F (71°C). Transfer the rolls to a cooling rack and let cool completely before storing leftovers in the fridge.

Serve: Plate the rolls with a side of lettuce and Nước Chấm or sweet chili sauce. Reheat leftovers in the oven at 350°F (180°C) for 10 to 15 minutes or in an air fryer at 350°F (180°C) for 6 minutes. Store the extras in the freezer. Reheat from frozen in the oven at 350°F (180°C) for 15 minutes, turning once halfway through that time.

Shrimp and Sweet Potato Fritters (Bánh Tôm)

This is a "jump out of your seat" appetizer to get them straight from Mom's stove. It consists of julienned sweet potatoes and shrimp coated in batter and then deep-fried. This popular snack, known as Bánh Tôm Cổ Ngư or Bánh Tôm Hồ Tây, was discovered on the street of Cổ Ngư, made with fresh water shrimp from Hồ Tây (West Lake) in Hanoi. Many people eat this with "Steamed" Rice Rolls (page 88). Using shrimp with their head and shell on adds to the crunchy texture when deep-fried and keeps the shrimp moist.

Yield: 4 servings

Batter
¾ cup (94 g) all-purpose flour
¼ cup (39 g) rice flour
½ tsp salt
½ tsp baking powder
¼ tsp turmeric powder
1 cup (240 ml) cold water
2 tbsp (16 g) cornstarch
1 large egg
2 tbsp (30 ml) neutral cooking oil

Shrimp and Sweet Potato
8 oz (225 g) large shrimp, deveined (shell-on or peeled)
½ tsp chicken bouillon powder
3 cloves garlic, minced
1 large sweet potato (about 8 oz [225 g])
Neutral cooking oil, for frying

For Serving
Fresh lettuce, mint, perilla leaves
Nước Chấm (page 178)

Prepare the Batter: In a large bowl, combine the all-purpose flour, rice flour, salt, baking powder, turmeric powder, cold water, cornstarch, egg and oil, and mix well. Let rest for 15 minutes.

Prepare the Shrimp and Potatoes: Pat the shrimp dry, place in a medium-sized bowl and season with the chicken bouillon powder and garlic. Set aside.

Wash, peel and cut the sweet potato into matchsticks about ¼ inch (6 mm) thick and 3 to 4 inches (7.5 to 10 cm) long. Add them to the batter.

Fry the Fritters: Fill a large, deep pot with neutral cooking oil to a depth of at least 2 inches (5 cm) and heat over medium-high heat. Working in batches—do not crowd the pan, or the temperature will drop—deep-fry the fritters at 350°F (180°C). To form a fritter, use a ladle to scoop up pieces of battered sweet potato and lower them into the oil, to prevent splashing, placing the fritters an inch (2.5 cm) apart to prevent them sticking together.

After 3 minutes, coat the shrimp with the batter and place one on top of each fritter. Spoon a little more batter around the shrimp so it sticks to the fritter. When the bottom is crispy, 1 to 2 minutes, flip it over. Fry until golden, 1 to 3 minutes. Each batch may take a total of 5 to 8 minutes. Transfer the fritters to a cooling rack or paper towel–lined plate to remove the excess oil.

Serve: Plate the fritters with a side of lettuce, mint, perilla leaves and Nước Chấm.

Pro Tip: Frying the battered sweet potato pieces first gives the potatoes time to crisp up without overcooking the shrimp. Resist the urge to add too much batter, or they won't crisp up.

Fish Sauce Fried Chicken Wings
(Cánh Gà Chiên Nước Mắm)

These crispy fried wings are tossed in a sticky, sweet and savory fish sauce that is lip-smacking good. They are the perfect Nhậu or beer food. Fried chicken has always been Dad's guilty pleasure ever since he immigrated to the United States, but this is a remix of home. Dad loves Popeyes™ fried chicken and listening to American '80s music on his speakers so loud that the house vibrates to the beat. My parents are as much American as they are Vietnamese, and I am as much Vietnamese and Chinese as I am American.

Yield: 4 servings

Chicken Wings
2 lb (905 g) chicken wings
¼ cup (60 ml) fish sauce
2 tbsp (26 g) sugar
½ cup (64 g) cornstarch
Pinch of salt
4 cups (946 ml) neutral cooking oil, for frying

Sauce
1 tbsp (15 ml) neutral cooking oil
6 to 10 cloves garlic, minced
1 to 2 tbsp (15 to 30 ml) fish sauce
2 tbsp (26 g) sugar
1 tbsp (15 ml) fresh lime juice
4 bird's eye chiles, sliced and seeded

For Serving
½ cup (8 g) fresh cilantro, chopped finely
1 lime, cut into wedges

Marinate the Wings: Pat the wings dry. In a large bowl, coat the wings with the fish sauce and sugar. Cover and marinate in the fridge for at least 3 hours, ideally overnight for best results. Remove the wings from the fridge 30 minutes before cooking, to bring them down to room temperature. In a separate large bowl, combine the cornstarch and salt. Shake the excess marinade off the chicken and coat the wings with the cornstarch.

Fry the Wings: In a large, deep pot, heat the oil over medium-high heat. Fry the wings at 350°F (180°C) until golden brown, 7 to 8 minutes. Do not overcrowd the fryer or the wings, or the temperature of the oil will drop. Transfer them to a cooling rack.

Make the Sauce: In a large skillet, heat the oil over medium heat and sauté the garlic until softened. Mix in 1 tablespoon (15 ml) of the fish sauce, the sugar, lime juice and chiles, and cook until reduced to a sticky sauce. Taste it and add more fish sauce, if needed. Turn off the heat.

Serve: Toss the wings in the pan with the reduced sauce, and top with the cilantro. Plate and serve with lime wedges.

Pork Meatballs in Tomato Sauce (Xíu Mại)

These Vietnamese meatballs are influenced by one of China's dim sum favorites, shumai dumplings. However, these are filled with onion and jicama for a crunch, coated in a umami-rich tomato sauce and served with toasted bread or rice. Although they're traditionally steamed, we're cooking the meatballs directly in this chunky sauce for an easy, one-pan dish that's equally plump and juicy.

Yield: 16 meatballs

Meatballs

1½ lb (680 g) 80% lean ground pork

1½ tbsp (23 ml) fish sauce

1 tbsp (15 ml) oyster sauce

1 tbsp (13 g) sugar

1 tsp chicken bouillon powder

½ tsp salt

½ tsp freshly ground black pepper

1 tbsp (8 g) cornstarch

1 tbsp (15 ml) neutral cooking oil

½ large onion, chopped finely

8 oz (225 g) jicama, or 1 (8-oz [225-g]) can water chestnuts, minced finely or shredded

Tomato Sauce

2 tbsp (30 ml) neutral cooking oil

1 head garlic, minced

½ large onion, chopped finely

3 oz (85 g) tomato paste

2½ cups (590 ml) water

2 tbsp (30 ml) soy sauce

2 tbsp (26 g) sugar

1 tsp chicken bouillon powder

½ tsp salt

5 Roma tomatoes, diced

½ cup (120 ml) water plus 3 tbsp (24 g) cornstarch, for slurry

For Serving

2 tbsp (2 g) chopped fresh cilantro, for topping

Baguette, or cooked rice and vegetables

Prepare the Filling: In a large bowl, combine the ground pork, fish sauce, oyster sauce, sugar, chicken bouillon powder, salt, pepper and cornstarch.

In a large pot, heat the oil over medium-high heat and sauté the onion and jicama until softened, about 3 minutes. This will add flavor to the meatballs. Transfer to a separate large bowl and let cool. Alternatively, add the raw onion and jicama directly to the ground pork later, when you cook the meatballs.

Cook the Tomato Sauce: In the same pot, heat the oil over medium-high heat and sauté the garlic for 1 minute. Add the onion and cook until caramelized. Mix in the tomato paste and cook for 3 minutes. Deglaze the pan with the water. Mix in the soy sauce, sugar, chicken bouillon powder, salt and tomatoes. Cook until the tomatoes are softened and the liquid has reduced, 15 to 20 minutes.

Cook the Meatballs: Combine the cooled (or raw) onion and jicama with the pork mixture. Wet your hands with cold water and form 1½-inch (4-cm) meatballs.

Taste the tomato sauce and adjust with more water, salt or sugar. In a small bowl, combine the water and cornstarch to create a slurry. Add the slurry and cook for 2 minutes. Place the meatballs in the sauce, lower the heat to medium, cover and cook for 10 minutes, flipping the meatballs halfway through that time. Now, lower the heat to low and simmer for 5 minutes, or until the center of a meatball is no longer pink and reaches an internal temperature of 165°F (73°C).

Serve: Top the meatballs with fresh cilantro. Serve them as an appetizer with slices of toasted baguette, or have them as a meal with rice and vegetables.

Green Papaya Salad with Shrimp (Gỏi Đu Đủ Tôm)

In Vietnamese, "Gỏi" means "salad"; "Đu Đủ" means "papaya"; and "Tôm" means "shrimp." This refreshing salad is sweet, sour and savory with a spicy kick. It consists of crunchy shreds of unripe papaya tossed in a tangy, fish sauce–based dressing, topped with poached shrimp, fried shallots and roasted crushed peanuts. Originating in Vietnam's neighbor, Laos, there are many variations in Southeast Asia, including Thailand and Cambodia. In Laos and Thailand, the salad is lightly pounded in a mortar and pestle, but for this recipe, we're using a quick salting technique instead, to draw out excess moisture. This will soften the papaya, allowing it to absorb flavor and retain its crunch.

Yield: 4 servings

Vegetables and Shrimp

2 lb (905 g) unripe green papaya

3 carrots

4 tsp (24 g) salt, divided

1 lb (455 g) shrimp, peeled and deveined

Dressing

1 cup (240 ml) warm water (110°F [43°C])

⅓ cup (67 g) sugar

⅓ cup (80 ml) fish sauce

¼ cup (60 ml) fresh lime juice

6 cloves garlic, minced

¼ cup (60 ml) sweet chili sauce

For Serving

¼ cup (10 g) fresh mint, chopped

½ cup (8 g) Vietnamese coriander leaves, chopped

¼ cup (15 g) Fried Shallots (page 180)

½ cup (75 g) crushed roasted peanuts

½ cup (8 g) Vietnamese coriander leaves, whole

2 to 4 bird's eye chiles (optional)

Prepare the Vegetables: Unripe papaya has a natural white, milky secretion, known as latex, when peeling and slicing into it. The latex has enzymes that can cause an allergic reaction to those with sensitive skin. Wear food-safe plastic gloves when handling the papaya. Peel the fruit, cut it in half and remove the seeds with a spoon. Shred the papaya lengthwise with a mandoline or grater, or by cutting it with a knife into thin strips. Peel and shred the carrots.

In a large bowl, toss the shredded green papaya and carrots with 1 tablespoon (18 g) of the salt, then set aside for 10 minutes. Rinse under cold water and gently squeeze out the excess moisture.

Cook the Shrimp: Bring a medium-sized pot of water to a boil. Carefully lower in the shrimp, inside a colander, add the remaining teaspoon of salt and turn off the heat. When cooked, the shrimp should curl into a C shape. If the shrimp is curled into an O shape, it may be overcooked. Scoop out the shrimp and optionally submerge them in a bowl of ice water to stop the cooking process.

Make the Dressing: In a small bowl, mix together the warm water and sugar until the sugar dissolves. Mix in the fish sauce and lime juice. Once cooled, add the garlic and sweet chili sauce. Adjust to taste.

Serve: Toss the papaya, carrots, chopped mint and Vietnamese coriander with the dressing. Top with the shrimp, fried shallots, crushed roasted peanuts, whole Vietnamese coriander leaves and chiles (if using), and serve immediately.

Pro Tips: Replace the papaya with other fruits and vegetables, such as cabbage, green mango and pomelo. If Vietnamese coriander leaves (Rau Răm) are not available, replace them with Thai basil or perilla leaves.

Beef Wrapped in Betel Leaves (Bò Lá Lốt)

As a 12-year-old, I still remember my first bite of Bò Lá Lốt and wondering why Mom didn't make them sooner! There were so many flavors foreign to my palate. Looking back, these experiences made an impression on my love for food. Traditionally, these are grilled over charcoal. The charred betel leaves release a smoky, peppery aroma with a subtle sweetness. Typically, they wrap around the filling entirely, but we used our home-grown baby betel leaves in this featured photo and couldn't wait. The North uses a pork filling (Chả Lá Lốt), whereas the South uses beef. Mom's secret is combining both beef and pork.

Yield: 6 to 8 servings

Filling

1½ lb (680 g) ground beef

8 oz (225 g) ground pork

½ large onion, minced

2 tbsp (9 g) finely minced fresh lemongrass

2 shallots, minced

3 cloves garlic, minced

1 tbsp (15 ml) fish sauce

2 tsp (10 ml) soy sauce

¼ tsp salt

2 tsp (9 g) sugar

1 tsp chicken bouillon powder

1 tsp freshly ground black pepper

1 tsp cornstarch

¼ cup (60 ml) neutral cooking oil, divided

40 large betel or perilla leaves

Pineapple Sauce (Mắm Nêm)

1 tbsp (15 ml) neutral cooking oil

6 to 12 cloves garlic, minced

½ cup (120 ml) water

2 tbsp (26 g) sugar

1 cup (155 g) canned crushed pineapple with juice from can

½ cup (120 g) fermented anchovy paste (Quê Hương Mắm Nêm)

3 tbsp (45 ml) fresh lime juice

2 bird's eye chiles

For Serving

Crushed roasted peanuts

Fresh lettuce, mint, perilla leaves, sliced cucumbers

Make the Filling: In a large bowl, combine the beef and pork with the onion, lemongrass, shallots, garlic, fish sauce, soy sauce, salt, sugar, chicken bouillon powder, black pepper, cornstarch and 2 tablespoons (30 ml) of the oil. Cover and marinate in the fridge for at least 20 minutes, ideally overnight for best results.

Make the Sauce: In a small saucepan, heat the oil over medium heat and sauté the garlic until softened and fragrant. Add the water and bring it to a boil. Mix in the sugar, pineapple with its juice, fermented anchovy paste, lime juice and chiles, and cook until heated through and slightly reduced, 5 minutes.

Assemble the Rolls: Trim the betel leaves, keeping ¼ inch (6 mm) of the stem, rinse clean, then pat dry. Place the leaves on a plate, the shiny side down. If using perilla leaves, place them on the plate purple side down. Depending on the size of your leaves, scoop 1 to 2 tablespoons (15 to 28 g) of the meat mixture onto the far, pointed side of each leaf, away from the stem end. Roll the leaf toward the stem, and wrap the stem around and tuck it under or through the leaf.

Panfry the Rolls: In a large skillet, heat the remaining 2 tablespoons (30 ml) of oil over medium-high heat and add the rolls in a single layer. Cook, rotating them to cook evenly, until the leaves have a nice char and the ground meat is cooked, about 8 minutes.

Serve: Plate the rolls and top with crushed roasted peanuts. Serve with a side of lettuce, mint, perilla leaves, cucumbers and the dipping sauce.

Pro Tips: Betel leaves can be difficult to find, but we've made this recipe with perilla leaves and really enjoyed that version, too. If you can't find either type of leaves, use the recipe to form meat patties.

These are also delicious served over cooked fine rice vermicelli noodle stacks.

Fried Pork Wontons (Hoành Thánh Chiên)

These wontons are filled with a seasoned pork filling and can be boiled, steamed or deep-fried. When I was in elementary school, Mom made trays for me to bring to class, hoping food would help me make friends. Food was her way of connecting to people's hearts, including her coworkers'. Her delicious food brought joy, but it was the thought behind her cooking and her gift of time that softened even the hardest personalities. I witnessed many tears at her retirement because of the impact she made. She showed me that being genuine was more important than worrying about stereotypes. "In life, some people just won't like you no matter what you did or didn't do." One day, I brought a tray to my best friend Jessica's house after school, and between the both of us, we ate all 50 wontons with Sriracha sauce.

Yield: 50 wontons

12 oz (340 g) ground pork

½ large onion, chopped finely

1 tbsp (15 ml) fish sauce

1 tsp soy sauce

1 tsp sugar

1 tsp sesame oil

1 large egg

½ tsp freshly ground black pepper

2 tsp (5 g) cornstarch

1 (50-wrapper) package wonton wrappers

Neutral cooking oil, for frying

For Serving

Sweet chili sauce or Sriracha

Prepare the Filling: In a large bowl, combine the ground pork, onion, fish sauce, soy sauce, sugar, sesame oil, egg, pepper and cornstarch. Mix the ingredients thoroughly in the same direction, such as clockwise or counterclockwise. This will facilitate the development of myosin, a sticky protein that will help bind the filling.

Assemble the Wontons: Place a wonton wrapper down, positioned like a diamond. Add 1 to 2 teaspoons (2 to 4 g) of filling in the center. Brush water along the edges of the wrapper and fold it over into a triangle. Use your fingers to remove any excess air around the filling. Pinch together the edges to seal securely.

Fry the Wontons: Fill a medium-sized, deep pot with oil to a 2-inch (5-cm) depth and heat over medium-high heat. Fry the wontons in batches at 375°F (190°C) until they are golden brown, 5 to 6 minutes, flipping halfway through that time. Be careful not to fry them for too long, because they continue to cook after being removed from the oil. Transfer to a cooling rack or paper towel–lined plate to remove the excess oil.

Serve: Enjoy the fried wontons with sweet chili sauce or Sriracha. To reheat, preheat the oven to 350°F (180°C) and bake for 5 to 7 minutes, flipping halfway through that time.

Pro Tip: As an alternative to frying, steam or boil the wontons as an appetizer served with chili oil and soy sauce. To make wonton egg noodle soup, try the Cambodian Phnom Penh Noodle Soup pork broth (page 63) served with boiled egg noodles, topped with the boiled wontons and slices of Char Siu Roasted BBQ Pork (page 119).

Vietnamese Popcorn Chicken Bites (Gà Chiên Rau Răm)

My Vietnamese twist on popcorn chicken uses a marinade consisting of fish sauce, soy sauce, brown sugar and garlic for an umami flavor. The potato starch coating provides a light and crispy exterior and the chicken is double-fried for an extra crunch to every bite. The bird's eye chiles and Vietnamese coriander leaves are flash-fried and add unique spicy, peppery and citrus notes. The hit of finishing salt and lime juice at the end cuts through the richness and brings all the flavors together.

Yield: 4 servings

1 lb (455 g) boneless, skinless chicken thighs

1 tbsp (15 ml) fish sauce

¼ tsp salt, plus more to taste

1½ tsp (8 ml) soy sauce

1 tbsp (15 g) light or dark brown sugar

3 cloves garlic, minced

½ cup (72 g) potato starch or (64 g) cornstarch

2 cups (475 ml) neutral cooking oil, for frying

½ bunch Vietnamese coriander

5 bird's eye chiles, sliced

For Serving

1 lime, sliced into wedges

Nước Chấm (page 178, optional)

Marinate the Chicken: Cut the chicken thighs into 1-inch (2.5-cm) pieces and place in a large bowl. Coat the chicken with the fish sauce, salt, soy sauce, brown sugar and garlic. Cover and marinate in the fridge for at least 6 hours, ideally overnight for best results.

Double-Fry the Chicken: Remove the bowl of chicken from the fridge 30 minutes before cooking, to bring it up to room temperature. Add the potato starch to the bowl and coat the chicken.

In a medium-sized pot, heat the oil over medium-high heat. Use a thermometer to monitor the temperature of the oil. Once it reaches 325°F (170°C), working in batches, fry the chicken pieces for 2 to 3 minutes, or until they turn a light-yellow color. Do not overcrowd the pot, or it will cause the temperature of the oil to drop. Use tongs to place the chicken on a cooling rack so it does not sit in oil. Then, fry the chicken again at 350°F (180°C) for 1 to 2 minutes, or until the pieces are golden brown and the chicken is cooked through.

Fry the Coriander Leaves: Wash the coriander leaves and chiles, and pat them dry. In a stainless-steel colander, lower the leaves into the hot oil for 1 minute, or until fried. Place the fried leaves on a paper towel to remove the excess oil. Use a stainless-steel strainer to lower the chiles into the oil for 1 minute. Remove the strainer and place the chiles on a paper towel to remove the excess oil.

Serve: Plate the fried chicken, bird's eye chiles and coriander leaves, and give everything a gentle toss. Sprinkle with salt to taste and top with a squeeze of lime juice. Optionally, serve with Nước Chấm.

Coming
Full Circle

Classic Vietnamese Sweets

When my parents eat Chè, I can visibly see that this dessert brings them back to their carefree childhood in Vietnam, eating a cup of sweet pudding, sitting on a stool by the road. Every time, they joyfully slurp down the dessert and remark how good it tastes, "Quá Ngon!" which means it is *very delicious*.

One day, I gave Dad a glass of Mom's homemade Chè and I caught him on the front porch, slurping it in silence. He scooped up the fillings with a spoon and had a wide smile from ear to ear like a little kid. It was beautiful to see him living in the moment, enjoying the fresh air and the warmth of the sun hitting his face. For some reason, this visual was bittersweet. I had flashbacks of my parents having worked their entire lives to care for us, and only now after retirement are they able to slow down and enjoy some simple pleasures. My parents never traveled, dined out or treated themselves. They saved every penny strategically for their children to thrive. Now that we're older and in a position to give back, they don't want anything but for us to invest in ourselves.

All they want is for life to be "Yên"—calm, smooth and peaceful—for their loved ones to be healthy, happy and safe. I think of them and I'm reminded to appreciate what's important: family.

Dad didn't have an easy life. He lost his mom to ovarian cancer when he was barely a teen. In between that and serving in the war, he had to grow up fast. Chè takes him down memory lane to memories of his mom coming home to surprise him with sweet treats when he was a kid. I didn't get to meet Bà Nội, my grandmother, but I could tell through his stories that her love for him was immense. She would have been proud of her son.

I asked Dad, "What's your favorite Chè?" He grinned and said, "I like ALL Chè."

This chapter features a "Make Your Own Chè" section because this dessert represents to me this new chapter for my parents, in which they are content and at peace, coming full circle.

Vietnamese sweets and drinks are reaching fanfare far and wide, from the world of Chè desserts to the Việt coffee culture. Desserts known as Món Tráng Miệng refers to food that cleanses the palate. The desserts aren't meant to be too sweet. Rather, they are a refreshing way to conclude a meal. Build your own Chè (page 157) or try making the Pandan Crème Brûlée (page 165) or creamy Vietnamese Caramel Flan (page 166).

Make Your Own Chè Bar

A popular category of Vietnamese dessert is known as Chè—a sweet soup, pudding or drink. The base consists of sweetened water, coconut milk or coconut cream with such fillings as beans, jellies, glutinous rice, fruits and more. Customize your own Chè by selecting the toppings and combining them with one or more of the bases and crushed ice. These recipes are for four servings, but can be scaled up for large gatherings. To serve, choose your choice of toppings and layer 2 to 4 tablespoons (see individual recipes for metric equivalents) of each selection into a glass or bowl. Add the base to bring it together. The order doesn't matter since it gets mixed together before eating, but I always put the coconut sauce last.

Yield: varies

Chè Toppings

Small Tapioca Pearls (page 158)

Sweetened Mung Bean Paste (page 158)

Sweetened Red Beans or Black-Eyed Peas (page 159)

Pandan Agar Jelly (page 159)

Pandan Cendol Jelly (page 160)

Red Tapioca Balls (page 160)

Cubed mango, black grass jelly, *boba*

Chè Bases

Coconut Sauce (page 162)

Sugar Water Syrup (page 162)

Avocado Smoothie (page 163)

Half-and-half or milk of choice with sweetened condensed milk to taste

Suggested Chè Combinations

Pandan Cendol Jelly Dessert (Chè Bánh Lọt): Pandan Cendol Jelly, Red Tapioca Balls, Sweetened Mung Bean Paste, Coconut Sauce

Three-Color Pudding (Chè Ba Màu): Sweetened Mung Bean Paste, Sweetened Red Beans, Green Pandan Agar Jelly, Coconut Sauce

Thai Fruit Cocktail (Chè Thái): Recipe included (page 163)

Avocado Smoothie (Sinh Tố Bơ): Recipe included (page 163). Serve with black grass jelly, Sweetened Mung Bean Paste, Coconut Cream (see Coconut Sauce, page 162)

Note: In the photo on the opposite page, the Chè shown from left to right are Three-Color Pudding (Chè Ba Màu), Pandan Cendol Jelly Dessert (Chè Bánh Lọt) and Thai Fruit Cocktail (Chè Thái).

Small Tapioca Pearls (Bột Báng)

These small, chewy tapioca pearls, also known as sago, give a fun bite to Chè. They are opaque but can also be colored either naturally or with food coloring for aesthetics.

Yield: 4 servings

½ cup (76 g) uncooked tapioca pearls
3 cups (710 ml) water, for boiling
1 tbsp (13 g) sugar

Soak the tapioca pearls in a bowl of water for 1 hour, then drain. In a small saucepan, bring the 3 cups (710 ml) of fresh water and the sugar to a boil over medium-high heat. Add the tapioca pearls. Simmer over low heat until the tapioca pearls are opaque, about 10 minutes. Drain, rinse under cold water and set aside. Serve the tapioca pearls with sweetened coconut sauce or half-and-half with sweetened condensed milk to taste. Add fruit like mango or combine with the other toppings. To serve, add 2 to 4 tablespoons (22 to 45 g) of the tapioca pearls to each glass or bowl of Chè with your choice of toppings and base to bring it together.

Sweetened Mung Bean Paste (Đậu Xanh Ngọt)

This versatile paste is used in many desserts and is one of the most commonly used toppings for Chè because of its subtle sweetness and complementary texture.

Yield: 4 servings

½ cup (100 g) dried split mung beans
2 cups (475 ml) water, for boiling
2 tbsp (26 g) sugar
¼ tsp salt

In a large bowl, rinse the mung beans until the water runs clear, to remove some of the yellow food coloring. Add enough water to submerge the mung beans by 3 inches (7.5 cm) because the beans will expand. Soak them for at least 4 hours or overnight. Rinse and drain. In a medium-sized pot, add the mung beans and 2 cups (475 ml) of fresh water. Bring the liquid to a boil over medium-high heat. Skim away the bubbles and discard. Simmer, covered, over medium-low heat until the mung beans are softened, about 15 minutes. Mix in the sugar and salt, and cook, uncovered, for 5 minutes, or until the liquid has reduced. Mash to your desired consistency or use an immersion blender for a smooth paste. When cooled, the mixture might thicken and get dense. Just add water to loosen it up, if needed. To serve, add 2 to 4 tablespoons (25 to 50 g) of the mung bean paste to each glass or bowl of Chè with your choice of toppings and base, to bring it together.

Sweetened Red Beans or Black-Eyed Peas (Đậu-Đỏ/Mắt Đen Ngọt)

Red beans and black-eyed peas can take a very long time to cook and soften without a pressure cooker, so we're using this canned version as a shortcut worth taking.

Yield: 1 cup (200 g)

1 (15-oz [425-g]) can red kidney beans or black-eyed peas
1 cup (240 ml) water, for boiling
½ cup (100 g) sugar

Drain the beans in a colander and rinse. In a small saucepan, bring the water to a boil over medium-high heat. Mix in the sugar and remove from the heat once it is dissolved and the liquid turns into a syrup, about 3 minutes. Add the syrup to the red beans and let soak for at least 15 minutes. If you want to achieve a paste, boil the beans with the water and sugar until softened. Then, mash or puree them. To serve, add 2 to 4 tablespoons (25 to 50 g) of the prepared beans to each glass or bowl of Chè with your choice of toppings and base to bring it together.

Pandan Agar Jelly (Thạch Lá Dứa)

Pandan jelly can easily be made with just a spoonful of agar powder that gives it the jelly texture. Create variations of jelly with the same recipe using different extracts, such as coconut. Double the sugar if eating the jelly as its own snack instead of as a filling in Chè.

Yield: 4 servings

1 tbsp (7 g) agar agar powder
2 tbsp (26 g) sugar
2 cups (475 ml) water, divided
¼ tsp pandan extract

In a small bowl, combine the agar powder, sugar and ½ cup (120 ml) of the water. In a small saucepan, bring the remaining 1½ cups (355 ml) of water to a boil over medium-high heat. Mix in the agar mixture and pandan extract, and stir continuously for 2 minutes. Transfer to a glass container or heatproof tray to cool. Store in the fridge for 2 hours, or until the jelly solidifies. Slice or chop up the jelly. To serve, add ¼ cup (73 g) of the jelly to each glass or bowl of Chè with your choice of toppings and base to bring it together.

Pro Tip: To make coconut jelly, replace the water with coconut milk. To make coffee jelly, add 2 tablespoons (30 g) of instant coffee granules to the coconut milk.

Pandan Cendol Jelly (Bánh Lọt)

These rice flour and tapioca noodles are chewy, sweet and fragrant with the pandan aroma. Chè Bánh Lọt can be enjoyed on its own or added to other types of Chè, pairing perfectly with sweetened coconut milk.

Yield: 4 servings

5 pandan leaves, or ½ tsp pandan extract

1 cup (240 ml) water

¼ cup (40 g) rice flour

¼ cup (60 ml) coconut milk

3 tbsp (39 g) sugar

¾ cup (96 g) tapioca starch

1 tsp neutral cooking oil

¼ tsp salt

Using a blender, blend the pandan leaves with the water. Strain the liquid and discard the solids. If using pandan extract instead, mix it into the water. In a medium-sized saucepan or small pot, combine the pandan liquid, rice flour, coconut milk and sugar. Over medium heat, cook until it thickens and the sugar is dissolved, about 2 minutes. Turn off the heat. Add the tapioca starch, oil and salt, mix until it forms a paste, then remove from the heat.

Boil a pot of water. Meanwhile, grease the inside of a piping bag with cooking oil so the paste comes out easily. Cut a hole about ⅜ inch (1 cm) across at the tip of the bag and fill the bag with the paste. Working in batches, squeeze 2- to 3-inch (5- to 7.5-cm) lengths of the paste into the boiling water. After 1 to 2 minutes, the cendol jelly will float to the top. Transfer it with a slotted spoon into an ice bath for 30 seconds so they don't stick together. Drain and set aside. To serve, add ¼ cup (50 g) of the cendol jelly to each glass or bowl of Chè with your choice of toppings and base to bring it together.

Red Tapioca Balls (Hạt Lựu)

These red rubies have a unique crunch from the water chestnut and a chewy tapioca outer layer that makes them fun to eat. Everyone in my family requests extra in their Chè.

Yield: 1 cup (200 g)

1 (8-oz [225-g]) can water chestnuts, diced

6 drops red food coloring, or 3 tbsp (45 ml) beet juice

2 tbsp (26 g) sugar

1 cup (128 g) tapioca starch

In a small bowl, combine the water chestnuts, red food coloring and sugar. Let the water chesnuts absorb the red food coloring and sugar for 5 minutes. Bring a small pot of water to a boil over medium heat. Transfer the water chestnuts to a colander placed on top of a plate. Coat them with the tapioca starch a little at a time. Use the excess starch from the plate to coat them again. Add the balls to the boiling water and use a chopstick to swirl it around to prevent sticking. In 2 minutes, they should float to the top. Transfer them to a bowl of cold water and give them a swirl so they don't stick. Drain and set aside. To serve, add ¼ cup (50 g) of the red tapioca balls to each glass or bowl of Chè with your choice of toppings and base to bring it together.

Three-Color Pudding (page 157)
Chè Ba Màu

Pandan Cendol Jelly Dessert (page 157)
Chè Bánh Lọt

ai Fruit Cocktail (page 163)
è Thái

Avocado Smoothie (page 163)
Sinh Tố Bơ

Coconut Sauce (Nước Dừa)

This sweetened coconut milk brings the Chè components together into a cohesive dessert. To make a thicker sweetened coconut cream, omit the water and omit 2 tablespoons (26 g) of the sugar.

Yield: 4 servings

1 (14-oz [414-ml]) can coconut milk

1 cup (240 ml) water

¼ to ½ cup (50 to 100 g) sugar (use less if preferred)

¼ tsp salt

1½ tsp (4 g) tapioca starch or cornstarch

In a small saucepan, combine the coconut milk, water, sugar and salt and heat over medium heat for 1 minute. Incorporate the tapioca starch and cook until the liquid has thickened. When it comes to a boil, remove from the heat. To serve, pour ¼ cup (60 ml) of the coconut sauce on top of the layered fillings in each glass or bowl of Chè.

Sugar Water Syrup (Nước Đường)

This syrup can be used as a sweetener for Chè fillings or to replace the sugar component in the Coconut Sauce (page 162) if you wanted to add milk instead, as an example.

Yield: ½ cup (120 ml)

1 cup (200 g) sugar

½ cup (120 ml) water

1 pandan leaf tied in a knot (optional)

In a saucepan, combine the sugar and water, and cook over medium-high heat until the sugar has dissolved. Add the pandan leaf (if using). Cook until the sugar water has thickened into a syrup, 5 to 7 minutes. Remove from the heat and let cool. To serve, pour ¼ cup (60 ml) of the syrup on top of the layered fillings in each glass or bowl of Chè. The syrup should be mixed with the fillings before eating.

Avocado Smoothie (Sinh Tố Bơ)

Smoothies are popular in Vietnam because of the local tropical fruits that are available. Mom makes this smoothie using the avocados that Dad grows in their backyard. The photo on page 161 includes black grass jelly, sweetened mung bean and coconut cream.

Yield: 4 servings

1 large or 2 small avocados, peeled and pitted

3 tbsp (45 ml) sweetened condensed milk, or to taste

1 cup (240 ml) or more milk of choice

1 cup (140 g) ice

1 tbsp (15 ml) fresh lime juice

In a blender, combine the avocado, condensed milk, milk of choice and ice. Pulse until smooth. Mix in the lime juice, adjust to taste and serve in a glass. Serve on its own or as a base for building your own Chè. To serve, pour ¼ cup (60 ml) of the avocado smoothie on top of the layered fillings in each glass or bowl of Chè.

Thai Fruit Cocktail (Chè Thái)

This is the easiest Chè to make and possibly my favorite go-to because of the combinations of fruit that feel refreshing. It is perfect to make ahead and bring to gatherings.

Yield: 6 to 8 servings

20 oz (567 g) canned lychees, drained and sliced

20 oz (567 g) canned logans, drained and sliced

16 oz (455 g) canned palm seeds or coconut gel, drained

16 oz (455 g) canned black or green jelly, sliced

20 oz (567 g) canned jackfruit, drained and sliced

2 cups (475 ml) half-and-half or warmed coconut milk

¼ cup (60 ml) Sugar Water Syrup (page 162) or sweetened condensed milk

1 cup (200 g) cooked Red Tapioca Balls (page 160)

2 cups (280 g) crushed ice

Combine the Fruit: In a large bowl or container, combine the lychees, logans, palm seeds, jelly and jackfruit in layers.

Make the Base: In a saucepan, heat the half-and-half with the sugar water syrup over medium heat for a few minutes until incorporated. Remove from the heat, let cool and pour into the bowl of fruit. Refrigerate for at least 1 hour.

Serve: Add the red tapioca balls before serving. Serve each bowl or glass with ¼ cup (35 g) of crushed ice or provide a bowl of ice at the table.

Pandan Crème Brûlée (Crème Brûlée Lá Dứa)

This dessert is a showstopper when you crack through the crust. Pandan is often referred to as the "vanilla" of Southeast Asia. Its grassy, fragrant leaves are subtly sweet but offer a unique flavor perfect for desserts.

For other variations, omit the pandan leaves. For a traditional crème brûlée, add 1 teaspoon of vanilla extract to the milk and cream. For a Vietnamese coffee twist, add 2 tablespoons (30 g) of instant Vietnamese coffee grounds to the milk and cream. Proceed with the same instructions to heat the mixture over medium-low heat.

Yield: 6 servings

Pandan Crème Brûlée

5 pandan leaves, cut into 1" (2.5-cm) pieces

1 cup (240 ml) whole milk

1 cup (240 ml) heavy cream

5 large egg yolks, at room temperature

½ cup (120 ml) sweetened condensed milk

Pinch of salt

¼ cup (50 g) sugar, for hardened sugar crust

Tools

6 (6-oz [175-ml]) ramekins

Kitchen torch

Prepare the Cream: In a blender, blend the pandan leaves and milk for 30 seconds. Stop and blend for another 30 seconds. Filter the liquid through a fine-mesh strainer into a saucepan. Squeeze out the remaining liquid with your hands. Add the cream and heat over medium-low heat until it barely starts to bubble. Remove from the heat and let cool slightly for 2 minutes.

Make the Custard: In a large heatproof bowl, gently combine the egg yolks and condensed milk. Temper the egg mixture by gradually pouring in the warm (not hot) milk, ¼ cup (60 ml) at a time, while stirring gently. This will prevent the eggs from curdling. Avoid mixing vigorously, or it will cause air bubbles in the custard when it cooks. Mix in a pinch of salt to the custard..

Bake the Custard: Pour the custard through a fine-mesh strainer, evenly across the six ramekins. Transfer the ramekins to a baking pan and fill the pan with hot water that comes halfway up the sides of the ramekins.

For 6-ounce (175-ml) ramekins, bake at 325°F (170°C) for 35 to 40 minutes. For larger ramekins, check them every 10 minutes after. The center should jiggle slightly for a creamy custard. If it looks runny and loose, it needs to cook longer. Remove from the oven, let cool, then cover and refrigerate for 6 hours or overnight.

Serve: When ready to serve, lightly blot the tops of the custard with a paper towel to remove any condensation. Use a spoon to sprinkle with just enough sugar to cover the custard in a thin, even layer. Start with 1½ teaspoons (7 g) of sugar and add more if needed. To create the crust, use a kitchen torch to cook the sugar at a low setting, or broil about 4 inches (10 cm) away from the heat source for 2 to 3 minutes. If broiling, make sure the ramekins can withstand the high temperature, and be careful, as the sugar can burn fast!

Pro Tip: Using too much sugar will cause the top to burn before the sugar layer cooks through. Using too little results in an uneven or soft sugar crust.

Vietnamese Caramel Flan (Bánh Flan)

This flan is influenced by France's crème caramel but uses condensed milk, which makes it extra creamy. For a silky-smooth custard, bake the flan low and slow to prevent the mixture from boiling, which can cause "holes." Mom makes flan for almost every gathering and pours prepared Vietnamese drip coffee on top. If you'd like a healthier version, replace the whole milk with 2% and reduce the condensed milk by half, using the same recipe and instructions.

Yield: 6 servings

Caramel
½ cup (100 g) sugar
2 tbsp (30 ml) water

Custard
2 cups (475 ml) whole milk

3 tbsp (45 ml) prepared Vietnamese drip-style coffee or cold brew, or 2 tbsp (30 g) instant coffee granules (optional)

3 large eggs and 2 large egg yolks

1 cup (240 ml) sweetened condensed milk

1 tsp vanilla extract

⅛ tsp salt

For Serving
2 cups (475 ml) prepared Vietnamese drip-style coffee, for topping (optional)

Tools
1 (8-inch [20-cm]) round nonstick cake pan, or 6 (6-oz [175-ml]) ramekins

Make the Caramel: In a small pot, combine the sugar and water, and cook undisturbed over medium heat until the mixture is a dark amber-brown, 5 to 7 minutes. Meanwhile, set out your cake pan or ramekins. When the caramel is ready, quickly pour the caramel into the pan or ramekins and swirl it to coat evenly. Set aside to let it cool and harden.

Make the Custard: In a small pot, heat the milk and drip coffee over medium heat until just warm and not boiling, about 3 minutes. In a large bowl, combine the eggs (both the whole eggs and egg yolks), condensed milk, vanilla extract and salt. Temper the egg mixture by gradually pouring in the warm milk, ¼ cup (60 ml) at a time, while stirring gently. This will prevent the eggs from curdling. Avoid mixing vigorously, or it will cause air bubbles in the flan when it cooks.

Bake the Flan: Preheat the oven to 325°F (170°C). Pour the custard through a sieve into the cake pan or ramekins until three-quarters full. Cover with aluminum foil and poke several holes in the foil so that steam can escape. This will prevent the flan from drying out and forming a skin. Place the cake pan or ramekins in a roasting pan or deep baking pan. Add hot water until it is halfway high up the sides of the cake pan or ramekins.

Bake for 45 to 55 minutes. To test for doneness, insert a toothpick into the center. If nothing is sticking to it, the flan is ready. The center should jiggle slightly for a creamy custard. If it looks runny and loose, it needs to bake longer. If it doesn't jiggle, the inside might be overcooked and have a more curdled, grainy texture. Remove from the oven, let the flan cool down, then refrigerate for at least 4 hours or overnight before serving, or it may fall apart.

Serve: Loosen the flan by running a knife along the edge of the pan or ramekin. Cover the flan with a plate and flip over to release it. If the flan gets stuck, rest the flan dish in a pan of hot water for a few minutes to melt the caramel before inverting it on a plate. Serve with prepared drip coffee on the side to pour on top.

Mooncake (Bánh Trung Thu)

In Vietnam, the Mid-Autumn Festival is called Tết Trung Thu, also known as the "Mooncake Festival" or "Children's Festival." My father-in-law was born on this cherished holiday, so we celebrate his birthday in style. Tết Trung Thu falls on the fifteenth day of the eighth lunar month, when the moon is at its fullest and brightest during the year. The full moon symbolizes unity, prosperity and family reunions. It is the only time of year when mooncakes are eaten in celebration of the harvest.

These elegant mooncakes are embossed with intricate designs. The square and round shapes of the mooncakes represent the earth and the sky. The outer layer is made of a golden wheat pastry dough, with such fillings as sweetened mung bean, lotus seed and red bean paste, plus salted egg yolk. The festival coincides with the end of the autumn harvest and marks a joyous time when families can take a break from work and spend time with children and loved ones. On this night, families gather in the lively streets and watch lion-dance performances while eating mooncakes and drinking hot tea under the full moon.

Yield: 8 mooncakes

Mung Bean Filling

1½ cups (300 g) dried split mung beans

3 cups (710 ml) water

¼ tsp salt

Scant ⅓ cup (40 g) cornstarch plus 3 tbsp (45 ml) water, for slurry

¾ cup (150 g) sugar

1 tsp vanilla extract

½ cup (120 ml) oil, divided

Store-bought cooked, salted egg yolks (optional)

Dough

⅜ cup (90 ml) honey or (99 ml) dark corn syrup

2 tbsp (30 ml) neutral cooking oil

1½ tsp (8 g) creamy peanut butter

1 tsp vanilla extract

1 large egg yolk

1½ cups (188 g) all-purpose flour, plus ⅓ cup (41 g) for dusting

Make the Filling: In a large bowl, soak the mung beans for at least 4 hours or overnight, then rinse under cold water. In a large pot over medium-high heat, combine the mung beans, fresh water and salt, and cover. Bring the liquid to a boil and skim off the bubbles. Lower the heat to medium-low and simmer, uncovered, for 20 minutes, or until the beans are tender. Puree the mixture, using a blender, until silky smooth, then pour through a fine strainer back into the same pot. In a small bowl, stir together the cornstarch and water to form a slurry. Add the sugar, vanilla and cornstarch slurry to the pot and cook over low heat. Periodically add 2 tablespoons (30 ml) of oil at a time and fold the paste, to prevent the beans from burning. Cook for about 30 minutes, or until the mixture has thickened and can hold its shape when folded. All the oil should be used within this time and the filling should be moist. Remove from the heat, cover and refrigerate for 15 minutes or overnight to firm up.

Make the Dough: In a small bowl, combine the honey, oil, peanut butter, vanilla and raw egg yolk. Add the flour and mix until incorporated. The dough should be moist, slightly sticky and easy to shape. Roll the dough into a ball and let it rest for 30 minutes, covered.

Form the Mooncake: Preheat the oven to 400°F (200°C). Divide the mung bean filling into eight equal portions and form each into a ball. Use your thumb to press down the filling in the center and insert the salted egg yolk (if using). Set aside.

Take the dough and shape it tightly into a ball with both palms of your hands. Spray the molds with cooking spray. Divide the dough into eight equal portions and form each into a small ball.

(continued)

Egg Mixture for Brushing

1 large egg yolk

1 tsp sesame oil

1 tsp milk

1 tsp honey

Tools

Mooncake molds (5.5-oz [150-g] capacity)

Roll out each dough ball into a 5-inch (12-cm)-diameter disk. Lay one in the palm of your hand. Add a mung bean ball in the center and tightly wrap the dough around it. Stretch it to cover any gaps and press together. Lightly dust the top of the mooncake with flour and insert into the mooncake mold. Use the palm of your hand to press it gently to fill in the empty corners. Remove the excess dough. Flip it over and use the handle to push down. Release the mooncake onto a baking sheet lined with parchment paper. Repeat with the remaining mung bean and dough balls, placing the formed mooncakes each 2 inches (5 cm) apart on the prepared baking sheet.

Bake the Mooncake: Bake the mooncakes for 13 minutes. Meanwhile, make the egg mixture: Stir together the egg yolk, sesame oil, milk and honey. Run the mixture through a fine strainer to catch any egg bits. Remove the baking sheet from the oven and spray the mooncakes with a mist of water. Let the cakes cool for 10 minutes, then brush on the egg mixture. Return the pan to the oven, bake for 10 minutes, spray again and let cool for 10 minutes. Brush with the egg mixture and bake for 5 minutes, or until golden brown. Bake for an additional 5 minutes. Transfer the mooncakes to a wire rack to cool for 1 to 2 hours.

Serve: The color will deepen and the flavors will develop further for the next 2 days. Wrap the mooncakes in plastic wrap and store in the fridge. Let the mooncakes reach room temperature before serving. The mooncakes will last for 1 week in the fridge or up to 3 months frozen.

Black Sesame Mooncakes: To make this variation, use the mung bean filling as a base, add 3 tablespoons (24 g) of toasted ground black sesame seeds to the mixture and proceed with instructions.

Vietnamese Iced Coffee (Cà Phê Sữa Đá)

This classic Vietnamese iced coffee is often characterized by its strength balanced with the sweetness of condensed milk. However, real Vietnamese coffee is made from the coffee beans grown in Vietnam, not just any strong, dark coffee. A Phin filter uses a slow drip method to extract the depth of flavor from the grounds. If you don't have a Phin filter, use your coffee maker as usual.

Yield: 1 serving

2 tbsp (30 ml) sweetened condensed milk

2 tbsp (30 g) coarsely ground Vietnamese coffee (preferably Robusta beans)

½ cup (120 ml) hot water (205°F [96°C])

Crushed ice (optional)

Make the Coffee: Scoop the condensed milk into the bottom of a glass. Place the Phin filter on top of the glass and add the ground coffee. Place the filter tray on top and twist, if applicable, so that it stays secure. Add 1 tablespoon (15 ml) of the hot water to bloom the ground coffee for 30 seconds. Proceed to pour the rest of the hot water into the filter until three-quarters of the way full, then keep pouring until finished. Add more hot water depending on your preferred coffee strength. Cover the filter and wait until it is done dripping, about 4 minutes. Remove the filter.

Serve: Mix together the condensed milk and prepared coffee. The color should change to a medium-dark brown. For iced coffee, add crushed ice.

Vietnamese Egg Coffee (Cà Phê Trứng)

Egg coffee was created in the 1940s by Nguyễn Văn Giảng while he bartended at the Sofitel Legend Metropole Hotel. Due to a milk shortage during the Indochina war, he mixed egg yolks with condensed milk, resulting in a luscious drink that resembles tiramisu. He opened the legendary Café Giảng in Hanoi, known for its egg coffee, which is still hugely popular.

Yield: 2 servings

2 large egg yolks from store-bought pasteurized whole eggs

2 to 4 tbsp (30 to 60 ml) sweetened condensed milk (I used 2 heaping spoons)

2 cups (475 ml) prepared hot or iced Vietnamese drip coffee

Ground cinnamon, for dusting

Make the Whipped Topping: A frother is not strong enough to create the whipped texture. Using an electric mixer yields the most gorgeous, fluffy topping. In a medium-sized bowl, mix the egg yolks and condensed milk until light yellow and airy, about 4 minutes. If the egg mixture resembles hollandaise sauce, keep mixing it further until it has stiffer peaks.

Serve: Add the whipped topping to your choice of prepared hot or iced coffee. Dust cinnamon on top.

Tom Collins with Preserved Salted Limes (Chanh Muối)

I asked Bách Trần, photographer, cocktail enthusiast and creator of @NhậuForever, to share a recipe. His photo features a "Chanh Muối cocktail" incorporating my family's recipe for salt-pickled limes, often used to make a savory limeade. The limes are preserved in a sea salt brine for at least one month. The sweet, salty, sour and bitter shines in this refreshing drink. It features Sông Cái, the first-ever Vietnamese gin, which uses foraged ingredients from the mountains of Vietnam to raise the visibility of its people.

Bách and I share a similar passion to preserve our heritage. His photography showcases the celebratory concept of the Nhậu life, capturing the spirit of community through food and drinks. His inspiration comes from the music and nightclubs of Vietnam in the 1960s, often referred to as the Golden Era: "I daydream of traveling back in time and visiting the night club that my parents worked at with a cocktail in hand, listening to Duy Khánh and Phương Tâm croon the night away."

Yield: 1 serving

Preserved Salted Limes
20 to 25 small limes or lemons
1 cup (288 g) sea salt
8 cups (1.9 L) water

Chanh Muối Cocktail
1 preserved lime wedge (from
4 edges cut lengthwise from 1 lime)
0.75 oz (23 ml) simple syrup
1 oz (30 ml) fresh lime juice
2 oz (60 ml) gin
Ice
2 oz (60 ml) seltzer
1 sprig mint

Tools
1 (1-gal [3.8-L]) sterilized glass jar, or
4 (1-qt [946-ml]) sterilized Mason jars,
with airtight plastic lid(s)

Preserve the Limes (or Lemons): Wash the limes thoroughly, scrubbing off any dirt and impurities. Pat them completely dry. Slice the top of the limes just enough that the flesh is exposed. Place them in a gallon (3.8-L)-sized sterilized glass jar or divide among four (1-qt [946-ml]) sterilized Mason jars.

In a small saucepan, dissolve the salt in water over medium-high heat. Remove the water from the heat and let cool completely. Pour the brine into the jar(s) and make sure the limes are submerged in the brine for preservation. If the limes are exposed to air, mold can develop. If needed, add a weight to hold down the limes so they are under the liquid. You can use a glass weight or small bowls.

Wipe off any remnants of the brine on the rim. Cover with an airtight plastic lid (not metal, to prevent rusting). Leave the jar(s) at room temperature for at least 1 to 2 months. Store the jar of preserved limes in the refrigerator for up to 1 year. Use a dry, clean utensil to remove them. Give the lime a quick, gentle rinse under cold water before using to remove the excess salt.

Make the Cocktail: In a shaker, muddle the preserved lime wedge. Add the simple syrup, lime juice, gin and ice. Shake for 10 seconds, then double strain into a Collins (highball) glass. Top with the seltzer and garnish with a sprig of mint.

Meyer lemons also work great for this recipe. These were picked from my sister-in-law's garden and fermented for 5 months. With time the liquid and the lemons (or limes) will also appear darker and may get cloudy.

Crushed roasted
peanuts

Pickled Carrots
and Daikon (page 182)

Peanut Sauce (page 183)

Pickled Carrots and Daikon
(page 182), finely sliced

Annatto Oil (page 181)

Scallion Oil
(page 180)

Peanut Dressing
(page 39)

The Essentials
Sauces, Dips and Condiments

What makes Vietnamese dishes special is the complexity of flavors and textures. Flavorful sauces, dips and condiments are just as important as the main dish! The right combination creates the perfect balance of salty, savory, sweet, sour and spicy. Make the Nước Chấm (page 178), pickled vegetables (pages 182), Fried Shallots (page 180) and Sate Chili Oil (page 181) ahead of time and use them throughout the month to reduce time and effort.

Nước Chấm
(page 178)

Pickled Carrots and Daikon
(page 182), thickly sliced

Sate Chili Oil
(page 181)

Fried Shallots
(page 180)

Nước Chấm with Tomatoes and
Pineapple (page 179)

Shallot Oil
(page 180)

Nước Chấm Three Ways

Nước Chấm Dipping Sauce

This quintessential dipping sauce and dressing is a staple in Vietnamese cooking. The magical combination creates a sweet, savory and sour sauce with a spicy kick. The base of Nước Chấm is a 1:3:1 ratio of sugar, fish sauce and water. For example, to make a smaller portion, you can mix together 2 tablespoons (26 g) of sugar, 6 tablespoons (90 ml) of water and 2 tablespoons (30 ml) of fish sauce for the base, then add minced garlic, lime juice and chile to taste. If serving this sauce with chicken, add thinly sliced pieces of ginger for a variation.

Yield: 2 cups (480 ml)

⅓ cup (67 g) sugar

1 cup (240 ml) warm water (110°F [43°C])

⅓ cup (80 ml) fish sauce

3 tbsp (45 ml) fresh lime juice, or more to taste

4 to 6 cloves garlic, minced finely

2 bird's eye chiles, sliced

Chili garlic sauce (optional)

White distilled vinegar (optional)

In a bowl, combine the sugar and warm water. Mix well until the sugar is dissolved, then add the fish sauce and lime juice. Let it cool and add the minced garlic and bird's eye chiles. Optionally, add chili garlic sauce and/or vinegar to taste. Taste and adjust as needed. Store the sauce in an airtight glass container for up to 2 weeks in the fridge, or up to 2 months in the freezer. If you put it in the freezer, fill the container only three-quarters full because the liquid expands.

Nước Chấm with Tomatoes and Pineapple

My mother-in-law makes a version of Nước Chấm with tomatoes and pineapple on special occasions, and it transforms this sauce. It is perfect to serve with Vietnamese Sizzling Crêpes (page 100) or Crispy Roasted Pork Belly (page 115).

Yield: 2 cups (480 ml)

1 tbsp (15 ml) neutral cooking oil

6 cloves garlic, minced

¼ cup (50 g) sugar

1¾ cups (420 ml) water

½ cup (120 ml) fish sauce

2 tomatoes

¼ cup (39 g) chopped fresh or canned pineapple

Juice of 1 lime

5 bird's eye chiles, sliced and seeded (optional)

In a saucepan, heat the oil over medium heat, then sauté the garlic until softened, 1 minute. Add the sugar and water. When the sugar is dissolved, mix in the fish sauce, tomatoes and chopped pineapple. Cook until the tomatoes have fallen apart. Turn off the heat and add the lime juice and sliced bird's eye chiles. Store in an airtight container for up to 1 week in the fridge.

Vegan Nước Chấm

For those who cannot consume fish sauce, use this vegan fish sauce dressing. Peanut Sauce (page 183) can also be used as a replacement for Nước Chấm.

Yield: 1½ cups (360 ml)

1 cup (240 ml) water

⅓ cup (67 g) sugar

2 tbsp (30 ml) light soy sauce

½ tsp salt

½ cup (78 g) sliced or crushed fresh or canned pineapple

2 tbsp (30 ml) fresh lime juice

4 to 6 cloves garlic, minced

2 bird's eye chilies, sliced and seeded

In a saucepan, combine the water, sugar, light soy sauce and salt. Cook over medium heat until the sugar has dissolved. Add the pineapple and bring the mixture to a boil. Cook for 10 minutes, turn off the heat and discard the pineapple. Once the mixture has cooled, add the lime juice, garlic and bird's eye chile. Adjust to taste. Store in an airtight container for up to 2 weeks in the fridge.

Scallion Oil (Mỡ Hành)

Scallion oil should not be overlooked as a topping. Its fragrant aroma adds a layer of nuanced flavor. Drizzle it on dishes for added flair.

Yield: 1 cup (240 ml)

8 green onions, chopped
½ cup (120 ml) neutral cooking oil
Pinch of salt
Pinch of sugar (optional)

Place the chopped green onions in a medium-sized heatproof bowl. In a small pot, heat the oil over medium heat until there are a few bubbles on the surface. Turn off the heat and carefully pour the hot oil into the bowl of green onions. Mix in the salt and sugar (if using). Serve immediately or store, covered, for up to 2 days in the fridge. Make the scallion oil fresh rather than storing it for too long, as it goes rancid quickly.

Fried Shallots and Shallot Oil (Hành Phi)

Mom's secret to flavorful fillings and sautés is using fried shallots and shallot oil for cooking. The key to frying shallots is patience. It takes time for the internal juices to dry out and for the shallots to get crispy in the oil. Low and slow is the best approach. Alternatively, you can purchase prefried shallots at the Asian grocery store, which can also save you time.

Yield: 1 cup (59 g)

5 large shallots, sliced ⅛" (3 mm) thick
1 cup (240 ml) neutral cooking oil
Pinch of salt

Pat the sliced shallots dry with a paper towel and separate the shallot slices well. In a small saucepan, combine the oil and shallots. Place over medium heat and cook for about 20 minutes, stirring continuously to distribute the heat evenly. If the heat is too low, they won't crisp up, but if the heat is too high, they will burn quickly. The oil should be steadily bubbling but not splattering. Adjust the heat, if needed, during the process. Once the shallots are a light golden yellow, strain them and reserve the oil. Gently pat the shallots dry and add a pinch of salt to them. They will get crispier once cooled. Store the shallots in an airtight container for up to 1 month at room temperature. Store the oil in a separate airtight container for up to 3 weeks in the fridge.

Annatto Oil (Dầu Hạt Điều)

This naturally red-orange oil has a subtle peppery and earthy flavor. It is ideal for imparting a beautiful red-orange hue to such foods as Spicy Beef Noodle Soup (page 57), Sate Chili Oil (page 181), Tapioca Noodle Soup with Crab (page 67) and more.

Yield: 1½ cups (355 ml)

1½ cups (355 ml) neutral cooking oil
2 tbsp (20 g) annatto seeds

In a small skillet, heat the oil and annatto seeds over low heat until the color is a deep red-orange, about 3 minutes. Periodically stir while cooking. Do not overcook the seeds because the oil will become bitter. Strain the oil, discarding the seeds. Let cool, then store in an airtight glass container for up to 3 months at room temperature.

Sate Chili Oil (Tương Ớt Sa Tế)

Once you make this chili oil, you'll be thinking about it as soon as it runs out! Add it to anything you desire. If you can't find lemongrass, replace with the same amount of shallots or garlic—whichever you like more.

Yield: 2¼ cups (535 ml)

2 heads garlic (½ cup [75 g] minced)
3 medium-sized shallots (¾ cup [120 g] minced)
6 to 8 stalks lemongrass, center-cut pieces (½ cup [34 g] finely minced)
1½ cups (355 ml) vegetable oil
¼ cup (14 g) red pepper flakes, or 8 bird's eye chiles, seeded and finely chopped, or more to taste
1 tbsp (15 ml) fish sauce
Pinch of salt (optional)
2 tsp (9 g) sugar
¾ cup (175 ml) Annatto Oil (page 181) or neutral cooking oil

Use a small food processor to save time. Process the garlic, shallots and lemongrass separately and set aside. Lemongrass can have a fibrous texture if processed in large chunks; be sure to slice finely, first.

Pat the processed shallots dry. In a large, deep skillet or medium-sized saucepan, heat the vegetable oil over medium-low heat (320°F [160°C]). Cook the shallots until the water sweats out and they start to turn light brown around the edges, about 10 minutes. Add the garlic and cook until it turns a light golden color, about 10 minutes. Add the lemongrass and cook for 3 to 5 minutes. Periodically stir the aromatics so they don't burn. Turn off the heat. Quickly mix in the red pepper flakes, fish sauce, salt (if using), sugar and annatto oil. Add more red pepper flakes if you're looking for more spice. Transfer the chili oil from the pan into a bowl and let cool.

The chili oil continues to cook after it is removed from the heat, so turn off the heat before you think it is ready. The shallots, lemongrass and garlic in the chili oil will crisp up further when the oil cools. Store in an airtight container for up to 2 months at room temperature.

Pickled Carrots and Daikon (Đồ Chua)

Without this accompaniment, a Vietnamese dish will seem lacking. Make a big batch of this and plan out your meals. If you can't find daikon, use jicama or additional carrots. If you don't have time, grab a bag of preshredded carrots from the store and make pickled carrots.

Yield: 6 cups (1.3 kg)

1 lb (455 g) carrots
1 lb (455 g) daikon
1 tbsp (18 g) salt
6 tbsp (75 g) sugar
1½ cups (355 ml) water
1½ cups (355 ml) white distilled vinegar

Wash, peel and cut the carrots and daikon into matchstick pieces, using a knife, grater, mandoline or julienne peeler. Place them in a large bowl, coat with the salt and let rest for 15 minutes, or until the pieces can be easily bent. The salt will draw out the excess moisture, which allows for better absorption of the vinegar solution. The pickled vegetables will also retain their crunchy texture. Rinse the carrots and daikon under cold water and gently squeeze out the excess liquid.

In a saucepan over medium heat, dissolve the sugar in the water, then add the vinegar. Remove from the heat, let cool, then pour the mixture onto the vegetables. Store in an airtight glass jar. The pickled vegetables are ready to eat after a few hours and can be stored for up to 3 weeks in the fridge.

Pickled Cabbage and Carrots (Dưa Bắp Cải Cà Rốt)

This is a great alternative to carrots and daikon, also perfect for eating with rice!

Yield: 8 cups (2 L)

½ head cabbage, cut into 1" (2.5-cm) pieces (about 1 lb [455 g] cut)
3 medium-sized carrots (8 oz [225 g]), peeled and sliced thinly
2 tbsp (36 g) salt
2 cups (475 ml) water
⅓ cup (67 g) sugar
1 cup (240 ml) white distilled vinegar

In a large bowl, coat the cabbage and carrots with the salt and set aside for 30 minutes. The salt will draw out the excess liquid, which will make the veggies crunchy after pickling. Rinse the vegetables thoroughly with cold water to remove the salt, and squeeze out the liquid. In a saucepan, cook the water and sugar over medium heat until the sugar has dissolved, about 3 minutes. Turn off the heat and add the vinegar. Pour the pickling solution onto the vegetables. Let cool and serve after 3 hours. Store in an airtight glass container for up to 3 weeks in the fridge.

Peanut Sauce (Tương Đậu Phộng)

The perfect peanut sauce is well balanced, creamy and rich, but also light. It shouldn't be too heavy or overpower the dish. Although peanut sauce is often associated with fresh spring rolls, this sauce can be thinned out and used as a vegan dressing for salads or rice vermicelli bowls.

Yield: 1½ cups (355 ml)

2 tbsp (30 ml) neutral cooking oil

3 cloves garlic, minced

½ cup (128 g) creamy peanut butter

½ cup (120 ml) hoisin sauce

1 to 1½ cups (240 to 355 ml) water, divided

Juice of 1 lime

3 tbsp (54 g) chili garlic sauce (optional)

5 bird's eye chiles, sliced and seeded

¼ cup (56 g) Pickled Carrots and Daikon (page 182, optional)

1 cup (150 g) crushed roasted peanuts

In a saucepan, heat the oil over medium heat and sauté the garlic. Mix in the peanut butter, hoisin sauce and 1 cup (240 ml) of the water. Cook until the sauce is homogenous and has thickened, about 3 minutes. Add the lime juice and slowly mix in additional water, ¼ cup (60 ml) at a time, until the sauce reaches your desired texture and taste. If you like it thicker, don't mix in all the water. Adjust the sauce by adding more peanut butter, hoisin sauce or warm water. Turn off the heat and mix in the chili garlic sauce and bird's eye chiles. If serving immediately, top with the desired amount of pickled carrots and daikon and crushed roasted peanuts. Let cool and store in an airtight container for up to 4 days in the fridge, or for up to 2 months in the freezer.

Pro Tip: For other variations, you can replace the water with coconut milk, coconut water or broth, and adjust to taste.

Mom's All-Purpose Sauce (Nước Tương)

This is Mom's versatile concoction used for marinades, stir-fries or to coat your favorite noodles. It is precooked, so you can use it for raw or prepared foods.

Yield: 2 cups (475 ml)

¼ cup (60 ml) neutral cooking oil

6 cloves garlic, minced

2 shallots, minced

½ cup (120 ml) hoisin sauce

¼ cup (60 ml) light soy sauce

¼ cup (60 ml) ketchup

¼ cup (60 ml) Shaoxing wine

1½ cups (355 ml) water

¼ cup (50 g) sugar

2 tbsp (30 ml) honey

2 tbsp (30 ml) sesame oil

1 tbsp (7 g) paprika (optional)

2 tsp (4 g) chicken or mushroom bouillon powder

2 tbsp (30 ml) water plus 2 tbsp (16 g) cornstarch, for slurry

In a saucepan, heat the oil over medium heat, then sauté the garlic and shallots until softened, 2 minutes. Mix in the hoisin sauce, light soy sauce, ketchup, Shaoxing wine, water, sugar, honey, sesame oil, paprika (if using) and chicken bouillon powder. Cook for 5 to 7 minutes, or until the liquid has reduced. In a small bowl, stir together the water and cornstarch to create a slurry. Mix the slurry into the pot until the sauce is homogenous and has thickened, about 3 minutes. Adjust to taste. Remove from the heat, let cool and store in an airtight container for up to 2 weeks in the fridge, or for up to 2 months in the freezer.

Acknowledgments

Má and Ba, we did it! Thank you for writing this book with me! I wanted to honor you and you just wanted to support me. Mom, saying that you poured your heart out is a vast under-statement. Everything I know, who I am and all that I aspire to be leads me back to you. Dad, you're my biggest supporter. You never hesitate to jump in and save the day, and you were by our side the entire way. Thank you for showing me anything is possible. I will forever cherish these memories together. Con thương ba mẹ nhiều lắm.

Tom, you're the love of my life and my best friend. I couldn't have done this without you! Thank you so much for being my constant rock. You lifted me up through this emotional roller coaster and were there for me 24/7, which wasn't easy. You rooted for me, made me laugh, and gave me strength when I needed it. I still find myself falling in love with you every day. I'm very thankful that I get to experience life with you and that we get to grow old together with our Gouda girl. Gouda, you make my heart full.

To my in-laws, Má and Ba, thank you for treating me like your daughter since the day we met, and for being loving parents to me for more than half my life! Con thương ba mẹ nhiều lắm.

To my siblings, Mindy and Maily, you've been incredible sisters and I've always admired you. Thanks for having my back and hyping your lil sis up. Alex, you are an amazing brother, and son to our parents. Kate, Lynn, Amanda, Art, Alan and Craig, thank you for loving me like your blood sister since day one.

To my nieces and nephews, Ethan, Emily, Angie, Alisa, Ryan and Erin, I'm so proud of the people you've become. Do what makes you happy and dream big.

A HUGE thank-you to the Page Street Publishing team! To my editor, Sarah Monroe Demchuk, you are BRILLIANT! I'm so grateful to have you as my editor and can't thank you enough for believing in me. Your guidance made my vision come true. Iris Bass, your magic and insight during copyediting was critical! Meg Baskis and Molly Kate Young, your tremendous efforts in creating this stunning design brought the words on paper to life.

To my besties, friends and 2S family, thanks for your friendship and continuously cheering me on. Jessica Uyên Hoàng, you are the most selfless person I know and went the distance to help me; thank you for everything!

To the community, VietnameseBoatPeople.org, The Vietnamese Podcast and Yôn Foundation, thank you for uplifting the Vietnamese people. Thi Đoàn, you're a beautiful soul and your artwork is transformative. Nguyễn Phan Quế Mai, your books evoke the power to understand, heal and embrace. Andrea Nguyễn, you paved the way for Vietnamese cuisine to be on the main stage. Everything Cookbooks Podcast, your outlet was so helpful as an aspiring author. Chef Jet Tila and Chef Toya Boudy, thank you for taking the time to share your words of wisdom with me; it means more than you'll know.

Finally, to the Share My Roots family, this book wouldn't be possible without your support! I'm touched by the outpouring of love, daily. I gave this my all and hope I made you proud. To my recipe testers and friends, you came through for me and I'll remember all of you: Christina Quach, Yasmine Nguyễn, Jenny Ha Nguyễn, Anita Hoong, Jessica Uyên Hoàng, Kim Trần, Vicky Tao, Julie Nguyễn, Helen Tang, Taylor Bảotrân Bùi, Vỹ Phạm Lệ Hoang, Elaine and Ken, Hồ Diễm My, Monelle Abaya, Iver Nguyễn, Nayeli Garza, Courtney McAllister, Courtney Alexis, Elizabeth Chua and Phương Lưu.

About the Author

Julie Mai Trần is a first-generation Vietnamese Chinese American who loves to eat, cook and travel. In 2019, she created Share My Roots, a blog focused on authentic and modern twists on Asian recipes with a focus on Vietnamese cooking. She shares her heritage through food, preserving stories representing the refugee and immigrant experience, in honor of her parents. Her aspiration is to encourage people to cook, connect people to their roots and shine a light on Vietnamese food, people and culture.

Her love for cooking is inspired by her mother, who showed love, compassion and strength through food. As a foodie at heart, Julie loves to experiment in the kitchen—whether it's making classic dishes or creating something new influenced by her favorite restaurants.

Visit her blog at: www.sharemyroots.com.

Index